Dazzle Camouflage

Spectacular Theatrical Strategies for Resistance and Resilience

Ezra Berkley Nepon

Dazzle Camouflage: Spectacular Theatrical Strategies for Resistance and Resilience

Printed in the United States of America
First Printing, 2016

ISBN 9780692595350

Design by Jai Arun Ravine
Cover Art by Jombi Supastar (Front) and Betsy Nepon (Back)
Photo rights belong to those credited in captions. Where no photographer is listed, photos were provided by the author.

Essays based on material in this book have appeared in the following anthology publications:

"Zamlers, Tricksters, and Queers: Re-Mixing Histories in Yiddishland and Faerieland" is included in *Transformative Language Arts in Action* (Rowman & Littlefield Publishers, 2014).

"Let's Get this Femme on the Record" is included in *Glitter & Grit: Queer Performance from the Heels on Wheels Femme Galaxy* (Publication Studio, December 2015).

This book was made possible through the support of the Leeway Foundation Transformation Award.

Contents

INTRODUCTION

In the fall of 2003, Ari and I cruised each other not-so-subtly as our paths crossed in a North Carolina bus station. We both looked too long, and longingly, while we each silently assessed whether the other was a teenage boy or—could it be?—another Jewish, boyish, *treyf* (unkosher) queer. We were looking for something more than similarity: a sense of kindred difference.

When we actually met a few days later at a queer artists' community in Tennessee, we laughed together about that sighting across a crowded room. This chance encounter illuminated just one more example of the ways that people (as we said) "from the same planet" seem to find each other, see each other, even call each other forth as if by radar. We came from shared legacies of queers and Jews, two cultures that each had devised intricate rituals of language and dress to let each other know who we are, even (and especially) in dangerous contexts. We knew that the too-intense gaze (eye contact asking "are you mine?") was one of so many strategies used to generate and cross into a shared space of otherness, both within and beyond the borders of mainstream culture.

When I talk about meeting someone from "my planet," I'm gesturing towards a queer sense of difference; the urgent feeling of "this is not my place, these are not my people—but my place and my people must be somewhere and I must find them." This book offers two profiles of artists that represent planets where I have found my people and place.

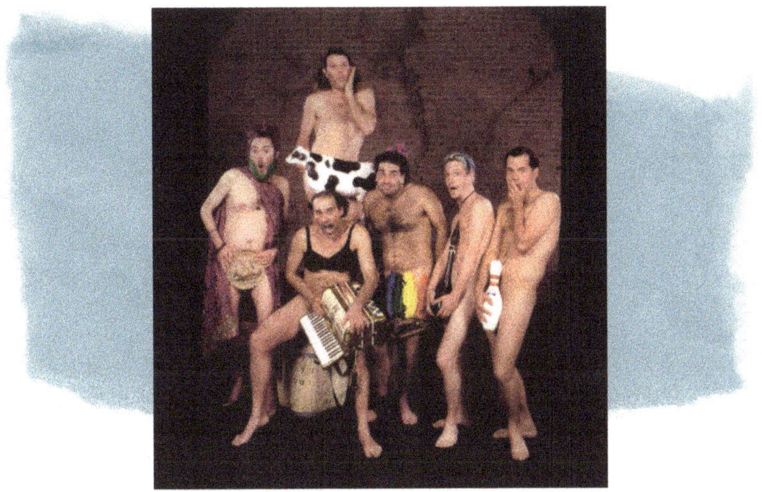

Eggplant Faerie Players promo group shot (EFP personal collection)

The Eggplant Faerie Players performance troupe developed out of Radical Faerie culture and HIV/AIDS activism. Their style of irreverent satire blends ingredients including clowning, camp, wordplay, and musical numbers. Headquartered within a rural queer community in Middle Tennessee, the Eggplant Faerie Players have been touring shows including *Person Livid with AIDS*, *Next Year in Sodom*, and *Welcome to Homo Hollow*[1] since the late 1980s. They talk about serious politics in ridiculous outfits, from Appalachia to Amsterdam.

While the Eggplant Faeries most often materialize on stages (and occasionally at protests and other events), the artists who make up the troupe have also contributed to building resilient and resistant culture off-stage, through their stewardship of intentional community and hosting creative arts-gatherings throughout the last two decades.

---

1   Sometimes called "Welcome to Homo Holler."

I met the members of the Eggplant Faerie Players in 2002 when I first visited their home, called Idyll Dandy Arts (IDA). In a short video documentary about IDA, MaxZine Weinstein says, "We end up putting on all these layers of skin, layers of denial about who we are, and we have to find places where we can peel off the layers. I can't imagine what's more important than learning how to be ourselves."[2] For me, I remember feeling something life-changing in the simple pleasure of just watching a person in high drag hanging laundry to dry in the expansive countryside—something about the difference between using decoration as celebration rather than as armor. I wanted more time with that feeling. I have visited IDA every year since that first trip.

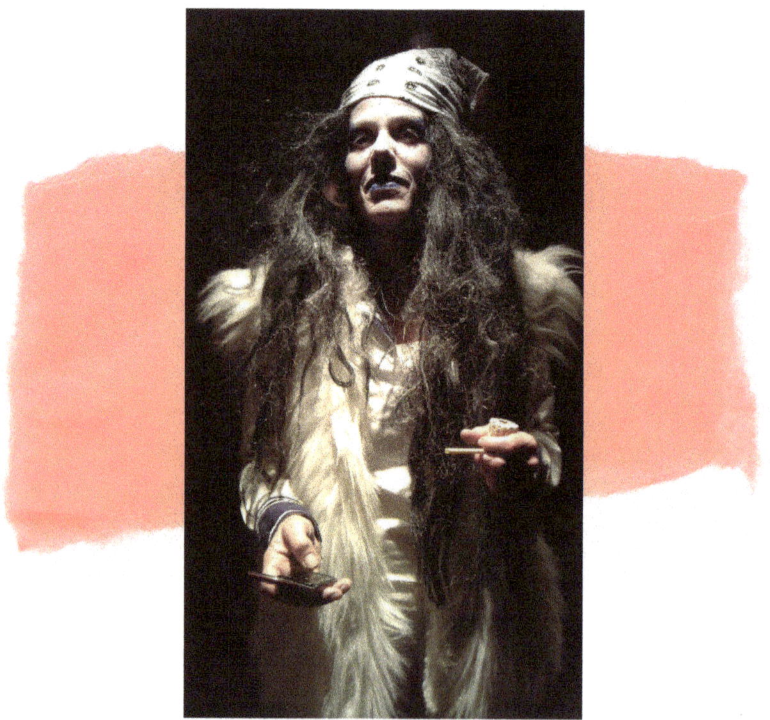

Jenny Romaine (Photo credit: Mor Erlich)

---

2   "Idyll Dandy Acres." *Vimeo*, posted by The Hussin Brothers, March 8, 2011.

Jenny Romaine is a theater-maker based in New York City whose specific brand of "ethnographic surrealism" remixes archival Yiddish sources with ongoing cultural exploration to produce avant-garde "New Yiddish Theater." Her methodology is informed by growing up in secular Yiddish Leftist culture, studying folklore and performance studies, learning pageantry skills with Bread and Puppet and the Ninth Street Theater, and then working in the YIVO (Yiddish culture) sound archive for thirteen years. She is a founding collective member of Great Small Works Theater Company, and longtime bandleader of Circus Amok. Jenny is the director of an annual Purimshpil[3] with Jews for Racial and Economic Justice, and the "grand maestre" of The Sukkos Mob, the KlezKamp Youth Theater Workshop, and many more productions of theater, street protest, and other spectacles.

In 2003, I co-organized a Purimshpil (a play in celebration of the Jewish holiday Purim) in Philadelphia: *Suck My Treyf Gender: An Anti-Imperialist, Anti-Occupation Cabaret*. Jews for Racial and Economic Justice (JFREJ) members Daniel Rosza Lang/Levitsky, Jesse Ehrensaft-Hawley, and Steve Quester came down from New York to emcee as the "Hadassah Ladies for Homos." The night had an alchemical quality. I felt my life changing, something shifting and then crystallizing, a kind of sacred meaningfulness in the super-queer, campy, politically radical, culturally-rooted, punk-rock Jewish theater that was also—for one night only—completely sanctioned by the Jewish calendar.

A year later I was in New York, where the Workmen's Circle's social hall was transformed into a queer dance party wrapped around a surrealist *shpil* (play) on immigrant rights. I was back on stage with Jesse-as-Esther, dancing and grinding and suddenly falling, sitting down a little too sharply on a divan. It was actually *the* divan from the film *Divan*, which traces the history of a Hungarian couch that was slept on by Hasidic *rebbes*, site of mystical visions and silent witness to atrocities. It was a crack heard round the world, ladies and gentlemen, the sound of the

---

3   Traditional play for the Jewish holiday of Purim.

most sacred thing in the secular room breaking. In the drunken chaos of Purim's frenzy, the show went on. But looking back all these years later, and still slightly guilt-ridden, I think: Wow, that was predictable. Isn't it our mandate on that upside-down night to break whatever is the holiest thing in the room, each year?

That's when I met Jenny, the honorable director of our Purim ship of Chelmish fools.[4] That year, 2004, she was co-emcee of the night with esteemed drag performer Rebbetzin Hadassah Gross (Amichai Lau-Lavie). The Rebbetzin entered in a dress made of prayer shawls while Jenny was decked out in leather miniskirt, giant two-tone hairdo, and necklace of crystal shards. She was a gothic force of nature and stage direction, informing the crowd:

> Hadassah stresses that on Purim, if you are confused, you are doing the right thing. She knows there are many paths towards holy disorder, many routes to the mystical place of misunderstanding. . . . The more we don't understand, the more dyslexic we feel, the more we are entering into the practice of Purim, the more we will be supercharged, renewed, transformed.

And so it was that I began to study Jenny's creative genius, thrilling to the process of being directed by her, and eventually coming to know her as a dear friend.

I'm drawn to these artists because they are people I love, and their work has been transformative in my own life. As a queer Jewish artist, when I met these culture-makers in my early twenties they demonstrated and modeled a path towards a creative life that actively undermines and opposes injustice. I learned from them as white people committed to racial justice; as people trying to carve out space for collaboration and collectivism under the boot of capitalism; as queer people with expansive vi-

---

4   The Wise Men of Chelm stories tell about a town where everyone is a fool believing themselves to be wise.

sions of gender and sexuality; and as radicals. I wrote this book because I wanted to know more about them and how they came to make the creative and the personal choices that have both impacted me deeply.

METHODS AT PLAY

The first time I heard the phrase "dazzle camouflage" was from my new friend Ari, the same-planet friend I first saw in that bus station. I knew intuitively that it described the way gender nonconforming people can use glamour, humor, and wit to create awe and excitement, distracting from potential attack.[5] As I came to learn, dazzle camouflage technically refers to a way of painting war ships: a crazy-quilt pattern of stripes and shapes that does not conceal, but confuses, making it difficult to tell the ship's location, speed, and direction. It's also a tool of the subversive artist, who may use surrealism, satire, camp, and other methods of spectacle to enable their message to reach even those who might be politically hostile. Dazzle camouflage offers both a way in and an escape plan.

The artists I profile here use dazzle camouflage and other creative strategies, include "remixing history" and "rehearsing resistance" to focus a strong political critique while keeping audiences engaged. Their work is weird and radical and super-queer, and it's also accessible—using "the three lavender shields of fun, friendly, and unexpected" to share their performances with a wide range of participants and audiences.[6] They take their performances to where the people are—on the streets, at conferences and gatherings, protests, community centers, schools— which allows them to reach diverse audiences without compromising

---

5   Ari Maxwell Bachrach attributes his use of the term to Lynda Barry's *Cruddy: A Novel.*
6   MaxZine Weinstein, "Radical Faerie Activism. Part One of Two," *AGENDA: Monthly Independent News and Culture around Ann Arbor,* March 1999.

their politics and aesthetics. In this way, they create spaces for people who share their politics to find each other and see our truths shared with the larger world, while also creating opportunities for wider audiences to hear their messages and join the fun (and the movement). When they find openings to reach wider audiences, they have a sense of "getting away with it"—getting away with subversive political agitation.

Their theater also offers participants and audiences tools to use in social justice movements—preparing us for revolutionary opportunities by rehearsing resistance. They teach us a song about police brutality that we later sing at a demonstration; they offer us an experience of gender self-determination worth fighting for; they share the devastation of the AIDS epidemic (or immigrant detention, or the bombing of Iraq) through a prism that lets us actually feel and process what we're being shown. They're not just telling us about political truths, they're training us; teaching us ways to witness, ways to act up, ways to fight back.[7]

Part of why I'm so compelled by these artists and their work is that they actively resist assimilation and "respectability politics." They critique mainstream culture, calling for radical change, and they bring their politics home, too. They dig deep into their cultural roots, not frozen in nostalgia but instead remixing history into a regenerating, evolving, vital radical culture.

Because of their anti-assimilationist politics, and their challenges to capitalism and business-as-usual, these artists' work is not commercial, and therefore not treated as "valuable" in mainstream culture. The Eggplant Faerie Players have been producing, performing, and touring shows for over twenty-five years, and Jenny Romaine has been doing the same for over thirty years. And yet, an Internet search in 2015 will bring up a surprisingly low number of show reviews (few of them recent) and only a handful of videos and interviews.

---

7   Here I'm referencing a chant from the AIDS Coalition to Unleash Power (ACT UP).

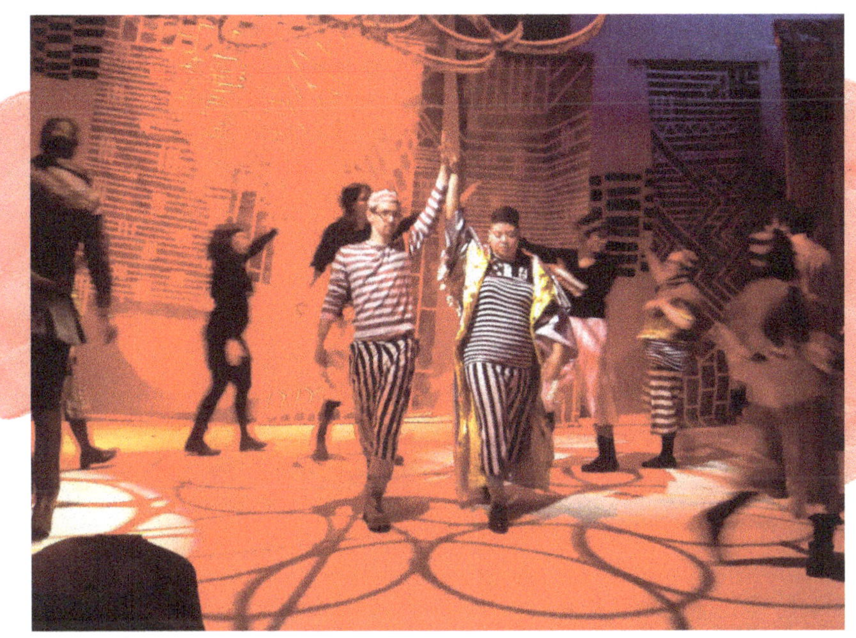

Rehearsal, Purim 2014

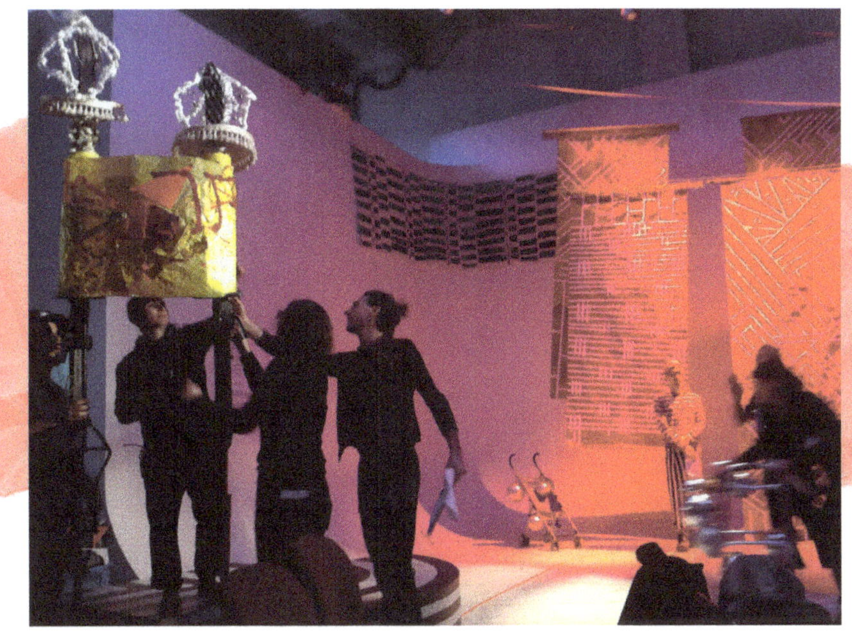

Rehearsal, Purim 2014

Though they had never met before I brought them together for this research, Jenny Romaine and The Eggplant Faerie Players are each artists with lifelong commitments to social justice. As a creative collaborator and community member, I have enjoyed witnessing and participating in these artists' work over the last decade. We are all, together, part of a large and intergenerational web of artists whose work shares influences, good friends and colleagues, political and historical context, and strategies for building transformative culture.

I wanted to learn these stories, and help to share them, because I know that precisely for the reasons they are not commercial, these artists' histories, archives, and creative strategies matter deeply.

In this research, I'm also asking questions about how these histories are archived, remembered, represented, and performed. I'm especially interested in what happens when researchers from marginalized cultures learn and write about our own communities, or those we descend from. I was excited by the possibility of honoring parts of our culture that often go unseen and unvalued when viewed by outsiders looking in with objectifying gaze. How do we move beyond invisibility, nostalgia, or objectification to build new, liberatory culture from our people's histories?

BETWEEN TWO WORLDS

In the writing to follow, I speak of the alternate spaces that these artists generate and work within as "Yiddishland" and "Faerieland."

Scholar Jeffrey Shandler describes "Yiddishland" as a place that comes into existence whenever two people are talking Yiddish,[8] the language of the Eastern-European Jewish diaspora—or, as Michael Wex calls it, "the national language of nowhere."[9] It doesn't exist on maps but rather it appears—is conjured—whenever Yiddish culture happens.

This framework can also be applied to the idea of "Faerieland," space created by people connected through Radical Faerie culture. The community of Radical Faeries evolved out of 1970s gay activism and counterculture movements, founded with a 1979 call for a Spiritual Conference of gay men joining together for collective healing, ritual, and liberation. Co-founder Harry Hay brought his radical politics and experience as a founder in the Gay Liberation Movement to the call, as well as his groundbreaking claim that a specific gay culture exists beyond individual gay sexual practices. Early Radical Faerie culture was also influenced by Arthur Evans, and others who studied the queer roots of pagan magic and envisioned a spiritual gay community. These two threads were woven into the founding of the Radical Faeries but never fully merged, and the tension between the Radical and Faerie elements of the culture continue to spark a dynamic and creative challenge as Radical Faeries have evolved into an international queer subculture. Faerieland, like Yiddishland, is a place with shifting boundaries, that manifests when and where Radical Faeries gather.

These conjured spaces do often feel to me like we are building what we call in Yiddish *"a shenere un besere velt,"*[10] a more beautiful and better world. I want to write about these lands and those building processes with all the love I feel for the generative spaces they can be. And yet, none of us enter these alternate spaces free from the harm and harmful training of mainstream culture. The truth is that just because you speak

8   Jeffrey Shandler. *Adventures in Yiddishland: Postvernacular Language and Culture.* (Berkeley: University of California Press, 2005), 33.
9   Michael Wex. *Born to Kvetch: Yiddish Language and Culture in All of Its Moods.* (New York: St. Martin's Press, 2005), 6.
10   The slogan of the Workmen's Circle/Arbeter Ring.

Yiddish doesn't predict that you will bring a desire for liberatory culture to Yiddishland. And being drawn to queer camping doesn't mean you are interested in unlearning oppressive behaviors in Faerieland.

All of the injustices and the liberation struggles of the world outside are also with us in these alternate spaces. Recently, I'm especially witnessing powerful critiques arise in these worlds about the ways that white supremacy and racism have played out in both of these (not-) utopian spaces. I see these subcultures being called to transform, to make the beautiful and healing parts of them just as joyful and re-energizing for all who enter.

These spaces are constantly changing—to me, they seem to change faster than the mainstream culture—and in the three years since I wrote most of this book, the artists and communities I'm talking about have continued to change, transform, try new experiments, find new collaborators, learn, struggle, and grow. These profiles serve only as snapshots, incomplete fragments of much longer stories. The stories are still unfolding.

On with the show!

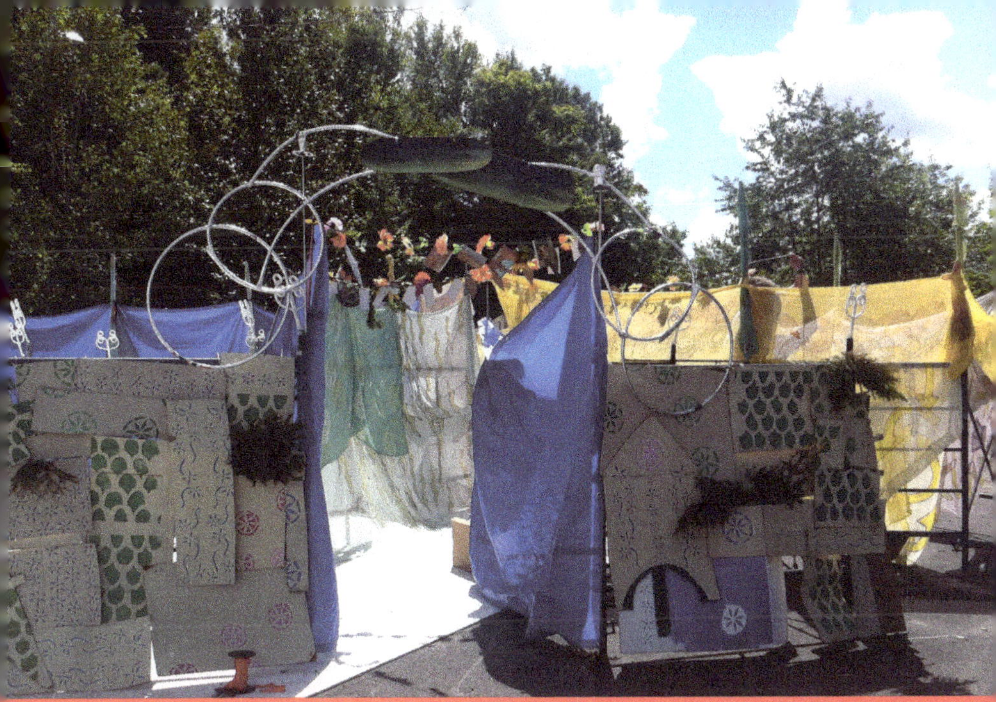

INTRODUCING JENNY ROMAINE

Building a Haunted Sukkah, 2014

At one in the morning, in the woods outside of Montreal, audience members filtered one by one into a dimly lit "Haunted Sukkah." Each audience member wore a mask made of a dictionary page with a sprig of cinnamon taped inside to heighten their senses. Performers startled and shuttled the audience from room to room of this maze-under-the-stars, each room holding new strange and shocking performances. These performances drew on stories of spirit possession from Yiddish literature, offered by scholar Agi Legutko: demon stories by Y. L. Peretz and I. B. Singer, and a haunting yet comedic film called "Genghis Cohn."[11] The performances and staging were also devised in response to archival Yiddish death folklore, and modern political writing about indigeneity

11   "Monish" by Y. L. Peretz; "The Last Demon (Mayse Tishovits)" by I.B Singer. "Ghengis Cohn" is based on the novel *The Dance of Genghis Cohn* by Romain Gary.

and language. Meanwhile, a live band led by Christian Dawid provided a suspenseful soundtrack by studying the horror-movie film scores of Bernard Herrmann and remixing Hermann's sounds with klezmer stylings.

As audiences moved through the haunted rooms, they were surprised by a demon jumping out from a bush, horrified by a preteen being hypnotized by capitalism and then cooked by a demonic princess, interrupted by a needy troll in conversation with a forlorn spider, and yelled at by a mysterious stranger with chicken feet, riding on a horse, screeching "Excessive use of force! Excessive use of horse!" The crowd witnessed a former Nazi soldier possessed by the spirit of a Jewish ventriloquist. They passed a giant snow globe with a shipwreck of Noah's ark inside.

With so much happening, so many complex creative sources and semi-random elements, Jenny Romaine's spectacular productions can look like chaos, leaving an audience member asking "What! Just! Happened!" But as I learn more about theater, as I develop my own work and experience other directors, I've come to understand that this seemingly seat-of-her-pants-style is a finely developed craft. Jenny's skill, training, and strategy are often presented subtly in the context of a constant feeling of experimentation and invention, but in truth she is consistently teaching us a developed methodology that addresses both the street and the stage, and aims to use ethnographic surrealism to transform our lives.

The story of how Jenny's skill, craft, method, and politics have developed goes all the way back to her great uncle in the Ukraine. In an interview with the Yiddish Book Center's Wexler Oral History Project, Jenny shared a story of her family's performance legacy:

My great uncle, may his memory be for a blessing, was an itinerant weight-lifter in small *shtetlach* [villages]. He would go from town to town having people dare him to lift heavy objects, and if he succeeded he got money and if he failed he didn't. So, this is someone I see as a professional task-based performer, and as a puppeteer and an object manipulator. I see this as: "Okay! In a Yiddish context, one lives, one breathes, one lifts objects as a profession." And so, he actually died lifting a horse. He ruptured his spleen or something. He died on a stage. All these things: the task-based performance, the object-manipulation, the horse, the death on the stage, I feel is important—a story that roots me in East European Jewish reality.

Interviewer: Do you remember what you thought of that story as a child?

JR: I just thought it was great, at least somebody is making money as an artist.[12]

A MOVEMENT KID

Jenny Romaine is a lifelong New Yorker, descended from a Ukrainian family of secular Yiddish-speakers, activists, and performers from whom she learned about the possibilities of social and political transformation. Her grandparents were part of the workers' struggles of Eastern Europe, and transmitted those values. "They had seen the tipping point," says Jenny, "They had been in revolutionary moments where they felt something much bigger than they ever could have imagined."[13]

---

12   Interview by Pauline Katz.
13   "Jenny Romaine on Shtetl." *Shtetl on the Shortwave.* 90.3 FM, CKUT, March 5, 2010.

Jenny grew up immersed in a culture of activists who had been members of the Communist Party and suffered from blacklisting during the McCarthy era. Her parents ran an anti-war group out of their house during the Vietnam War, and surrounded themselves with a community of organizers who had a practiced method to bring about change:

> It wasn't like you dream about it, and you long for it. It was like *you do it*! You go to meetings, you make things happen. You apply pressure, you use strategy, you work from a place of political love, and you transform the culture. With other people. *Given.*[14]

She grew up hearing Yiddish—she calls herself "a native listener"—in a culture of people who were "warm and funny and sensual and political." Jenny attended a Yiddish elementary school[15] and remembers learning about politics there, too, including a formative conversation about apartheid that modeled critical analysis as a Jewish learning value. Jenny understood early that "to be a Jew was to be engaged in larger discussions of marginality and power and who ends up on what side of it and what you can do to make justice happen."[16]

Jenny grew up in a secular culture that was informed about Jewish religious life. In an interview with historian (and friend) Rachel Mattson, Jenny explained:

> My grandparents would say, "We will now *not* say a *shehekianu*"[17] And that's the kind of secular Jew I want to be—knowledgeable. I'm not saying I don't love the tradition. It's just that I'm not a believer. People who live an Orthodox lifestyle don't own the tradition.[18]

---

14   Interview by Pauline Katz..
15   North Shore Kindershule.
16   "Jenny Romaine on Shtetl."
17   Jewish prayer in thanks for new and unusual experiences.
18   Rachel Mattson, "What Can Jewish Be?" *JBooks.com.*

Performance culture was also part of Jenny's home life from an early age. Jenny's mother is a longtime actress, television host, and arts activist, and her father was a member of the Jewish Young Folksingers. Jenny's first creative training was in dance. She was a professional-level dancer throughout her teens, with a rigorous practice: taking classes every day, often dancing nine hours a day. She took classes with Marjorie Mussman, dancing alongside ballerinas from the Cleveland Ballet, Mark Morris, Madonna, everyone in New York. She reflects that the dance class environment is very interesting because "You're with a group of people, you work very hard for two hours, you watch each other, and you see each other develop. You have these lovely relationships with hundreds of people, and you're familiar with their bodies and how they move."

Themes from this training have continued throughout her creative life: rigorous practice, collective creative culture, and movement-based performance—Jenny connects her dance training to her later work in puppetry because dance is all about "how things move."

Despite her professional training, the body politics in the dance world pushed her away from the conservatory college track. She attended college part-time at NYU while continuing to take dance classes and studying experimental theater with Ann Bogart. At NYU, Jenny also took a folklore class taught by Barbara Kirshenblatt-Gimblett, on "The Aesthetics of Everyday Life," a class that she says "shaped everything I did for the rest of my life."

As soon as Jenny started at NYU, she got involved with Women's Pentagon Action (WPA). This group of "powerhouse feminists" included activists like Grace Paley, Vera Williams, Blue London, Vicky Revere, Kady Van Deurs, Jan Clausen. . . . Jenny remembers, "I was a movement kid, so going to the Women's Pentagon Action I was like 'Oh my God, here they are!'" At eighteen, she was among the youngest members and she was in a working group with Ann-christine d'Adesky, (now Rabbi) Sharon Kleinbaum, Laura Flanders . . . "all these people who later became big leaders, wearing overalls and having intense political discussions."

The big direct action they were planning took place on November 17th, 1980 in Washington, DC and brought together women from across the US and Canada. They gathered to protest military expansion and cuts to social services, and they joined in an intersectional agenda set out in the Unity Statement written by Grace Paley. Artist and activist Amy Trompetter had made four giant puppets representing the four stages of the demonstration: one woman in black representing mourning, one in red for rage, one in yellow for empowerment, and one in white symbolizing defiance. This was the first time Jenny had seen giant puppets and she was blown away. Protesters marched from Arlington Cemetery to the grounds of the Pentagon, where they set up a cemetery for all the women killed because of militarism. In the final stage of the action, protesters knitted the Pentagon doors together with webs of yarn, weaving themselves into the webs, shutting it down. Jenny spent two weeks in the Federal Correctional Institution in Alderson, West Virginia after being arrested at that action, going to meetings and political discussions every day with the WPA arrestees and the other inmates.

Many of the powerhouse activists in Women's Pentagon Action were also lesbians, and that was new for Jenny. She remembers being scared about what it meant for her to be exposed to all this "lesbian possibility." She met her first girlfriend through WPA. This brought her into community with a culture of women passionate about dyke visibility. The women she met went on to found DYKE TV, and the Lesbian Avengers, and to play crucial roles in ACT UP, Queer Nation, and beyond.

ALL PUPPETS, GREAT AND SMALL

Seeing that Jenny was so thrilled by the giant puppets at the 1980 Women's Pentagon Action, Grace Paley sent her to spend the next summer with Bread and Puppet Theater (B&P), which Jenny calls a "total world changer."

From the age of nineteen into her early twenties, Jenny learned a craft of avant-garde folk art from Bread and Puppet, a style that she describes using words like open, prismatic, weird, handmade, socially engaged, abstract, populist, "never cutesy-nostalgic," and "in the landscape."[19]

Peter Schumann founded Bread and Puppet in 1963 in NYC's Lower East Side,[20] a performance company that became known for creating huge protest puppet processions and holiday celebrations. In 1974, the company moved to Glover, VT and hosted an annual Domestic Resurrection Circus there, also building a puppet museum and touring shows around the US and abroad.[21]

The B&P community was intergenerational, and Jenny gathered that a strong, vibrant alternative culture must have a wide range of ages working together—with a clear and honored role for youth and elders—a val-

---

19   Interview by Pauline Katz.
20   Just a few years later, John Vaccaro would create the Theatre of the Ridiculous in the same neighborhood.
21   "Bread and Puppet: Cheap Art and Political Theater," from http://breadandpuppet. org.

ue that continues to inform her work. But it wasn't all good—Jenny was shocked to find a patriarchal culture at Bread and Puppet.

> This is when Peter was doing these giant shows with hundreds of people in the landscape and lighting things on fire and the art was *off the hook* but it was like, *where are the women? Where is the feminism?*
>
> I can't tell you how much the art affected me, it totally shaped everything I am. But there was all this sexism! Women using tools? Women weren't getting up on ladders. I mean, in the world I came from it was the opposite! There were very few men in my life. So I was like, "Grace, how can you send me here?" But it was still so clear to me there was so much to learn there, and I found my niche.

When Jenny came back from Bread and Puppet, she started working with Ninth Street Theater—with Joanne Schultz, Ralph Denzer, Ron Kelly and others in Bread & Puppet's New York auxiliary crew. She worked with Ninth Street Theater for ten years and also worked as a stilt dancer, busking and doing gigs with their On the Lam Street Band.

This creative partnership was a training ground and apprenticeship—Jenny learned the crafts of theater production, street spectacle, and radical brass bands. She also learned a leaderless collective model of ensemble cultural production, a different structure than she had been exposed to in the dance world, more aligned with grassroots political organizing.

In 1991, Jenny co-founded Great Small Works (GSW), "a collective of artists who keep theater at the heart of social life," with Ninth Street Theater/Bread and Puppet colleagues John Bell, Trudi Cohen, Stephen Kaplan, Roberto Rossi, and Mark Sussman. Still going strong today, Great Small Works uses a wide range of puppet theater models, including giant puppets, masks, contestoria, processions and parades, and toy theater productions. Their first show was called *The Toy Theater of Terror As Usual*, intended as a response to saber-rattling media messages in anticipation of the Gulf War. Referencing Walter Benjamin's notion of culture in a permanent "state of emergency" and the political collages of Weimar artist John Heartfield, GSW created a "surreal news serial." This montage-in-motion presented moving images and text from newspapers, magazines, and philosophical works, manipulated by five puppeteers behind a tabletop proscenium stage.[22]

"We were interested in remixing the news," says Jenny:

> It was during the first Gulf War, the first time the United States invaded Iraq, and we were getting this monstrous newsfeed. This was at a time when people read newspapers, and many urban people were reading the same urban newspapers. So we thought "we really want to make our own news reels and remix this imagery, and push back." I mean, we were involved in all kinds of other political demonstrations, but this was a way to respond as artists.[23]

The art form of toy theater provided a format for re-mixing history, and simultaneously an opportunity to imagine a new kind of media messaging—rehearsing resistance in a miniature version. Great Small Works' John Bell talks about "the compressed power of the miniature" as an agent of transformation:

> By scaling something down, we fundamentally change it. It's not just a smaller version of the original, it's a different object altogether: in a new environment; with new relationships to the world; all the rules have changed. A bird is bigger than a person is bigger than a skyscraper. A coke bottle encloses a boat (and a

22   http://greatsmallworks.org/festivals-spaghetti/index.html
23   "Jenny Romaine on Shtetl."

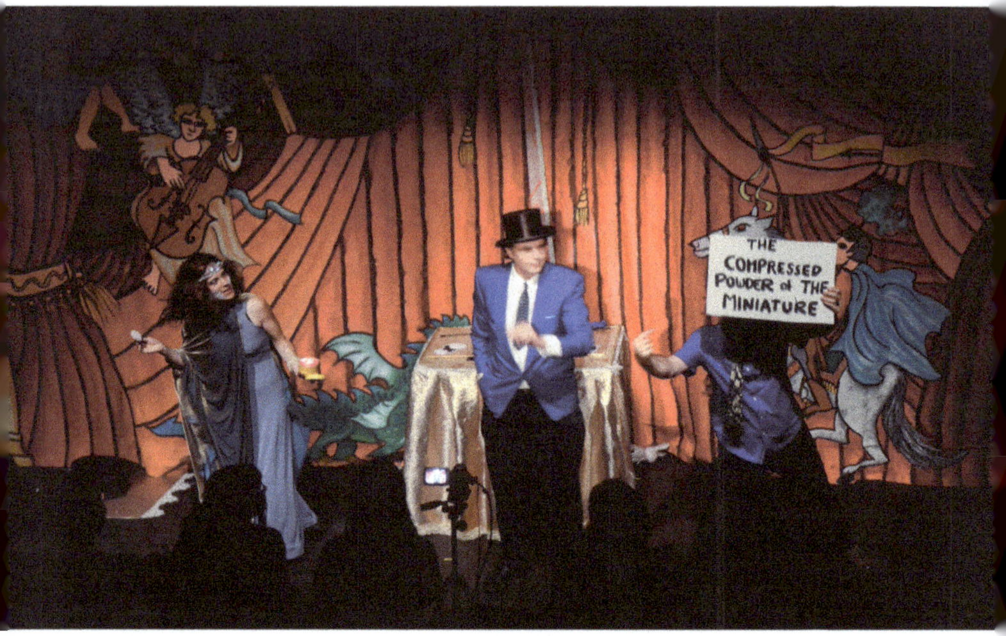

Great Small Works Toy Theater Festival, 2013 (Photo credit: Minister Erik McGregor)

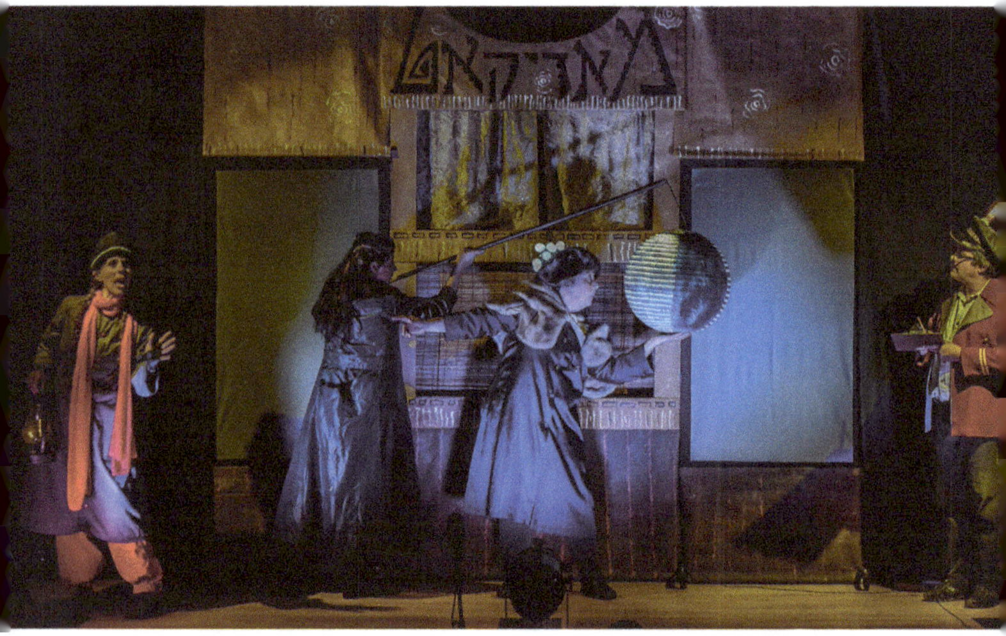

Great Small Works, The Modicut Project: World Premiere - Rehearsal, 2015
(Photo credit: Minister Erik McGregor)

Coming out of the massive puppetry and moving spectacles of Bread and Puppet's rolling Vermont landscape, toy theater was also a strategy that reflected the budget and space concerns of making work in the gentrifying Lower East Side. GSW has utilized this affordable, transportable Victorian theater style to bring shows into schools, prisons, libraries, streets, theaters, and living rooms for over two decades, helping to repopularize the form. Since 1993, GSW has produced a semi-annual Toy Theater Festival and has toured internationally with toy theater performances, exhibits, and workshops.[25]

Spaghetti Dinners are another GSW element, with roots in the Bread and Puppet practice of serving fresh-baked bread along with the show.[26] Great Small Works' semi-monthly night of pasta and performance serves as a place to workshop new shows, showcase productions by traveling puppeteers and other artists, and as a dependable gathering site for celebrating annual festivals and holidays in GSW's wonderful, weird, and warm creative community.

The stories of Ninth Street Theater and Great Small Works tie into the history of gentrification in Manhattan and Brooklyn. The groups' workshops and the monthly Spaghetti Dinner events[27] started in an East 9th Street storefront on the Lower East Side and stayed there until 1984, when they were forced out in a wave of gentrification. They landed at Charas/El Bohio, a center of visionary Nuyorican community organizing in Loisaida (the Lower East Side).[28] After a long fight of community orga-

---

24   John Bell. "The Miniature a Sprout Spaghetti Dinner." *Vimeo* video.
25   "Great Small Works: Introduction, History, and Company Bios," from Great Small Works, http://www.greatsmallworks.org/pages/about_the_company.html#history.
26   Gary Shapiro. "Great Small Works Moves From P.S. 122." *The New York Sun.* http://www.nysun.com/arts/great-small-works-moves-from-ps-122/25579.
27   Originally "Pasta and Puppets," started by Amy Trompetter.
28   Armando Perez and Chino Garcia, co-founders of the Charas/El Bohio Cultural Community Center had a connection to Goddard College and had encountered Bread

nizing to resist displacement, New York City Mayor Rudy Giuliani shut down Charas/El Bohio at the end of 2001. Great Small Works moved to Brooklyn's DUMBO neighborhood.[29] Meanwhile, the Spaghetti Dinners moved to downtown Manhattan performance space PS122. Eventually they had to leave PS122, and the dinners now happen at Judson Church near Washington Square Park. Since moving to DUMBO, the GSW studio has been forced to move multiple times because of gentrification.

These are just a few examples of the struggle for creative space amidst waves of gentrification and displacement—part of a much bigger story about the impact of gentrification on communities in New York since the 1980s.

QUEER DIRECT ACTION

Though Jenny's main creative communities—Bread and Puppet, the Ninth Street Theater, and Great Small Works—were not queer groups, they performed at Theater for the New City and other experimental theater venues along with all the queer performance artists like the Bloolips, and the Ridiculous Theater Company.[30] Jenny remembers, "I would always be seeing Ethyl Eichelberger's ass, in stilettos, changing her clothes at the street fairs."[31]

---

and Puppet through Goddard; that's how they had a sense of Great Small Works' political affiliation and how GSW ended up working out of Charas/El Bohio.
29   DUMBO = Down Under the Manhattan Bridge.
30   Jenny was also around the WOW scene of feminist theater that came together in the early 1980s, but at the time she found herself intimidated by actors, more comfortable with puppeteers ("who wear bags over their heads").
31   Ethyl Eichelberger (1945-90) was a performer, playwright, accordion-player, wig-maker and fabulous art-freak who was also a member of Charles Ludlam's Ridiculous Theater Company as well as performing on Broadway and television. For more on Eichelberger, see Joe E. Jeffreys, "An Outre Entree into the Para-ridiculous Histrionics of Drag Diva Ethyl Eichelberger: A True Story" (PhD diss., New York University, 1996).

She wasn't only working adjacent to queer performance, she was also an active participant in multiple 1990s-era queer movements for visibility and justice. Often, this took the form of organizing and playing in marching bands for direct actions, drawing on her street theater experience, as in her role as bandleader for Circus Amok, in close partnership with long-time collaborator Jennifer Miller.

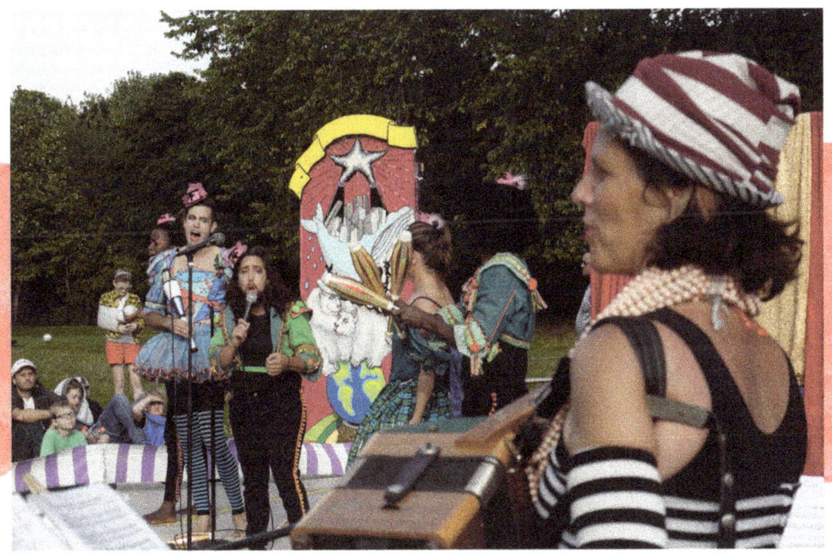

Jenny Romaine [right] with Circus Amok (Photo credit: Virginie Danglades)

A documentary video clip of the Lesbian Avengers' first direct action in September 1992 opens with Jenny's voice:

> Ladies and ladies, gentlemen and gentlemen! We are! The Lesbian Avengers! Here to ensure the visibility and survival of lesbians everywhere! And now: a number we wrote for the first day of school. It's kind of a polka. A lesbian polka!"[32]

Jenny wears a giant drum and carries a drumstick in one hand and a cymbal in the other. Crash! Bang! Commence "This Land is Your Land" sung with new lyrics, a marching band leading a crew of dykes through

---

32   "Back to School with the Lesbian Avengers, 1992." YouTube video. http://www.youtube.com/watch?v=dzIbGdP7MDQ.

Queens wearing "I was a lesbian child" T-shirts and carrying purple balloons printed with "Ask About Lesbian Lives" that they will give away to school children to protest the school board's decision to ban a multicultural curriculum called "Children of the Rainbow."

Jenny organized the band for this action, and she dressed them in kilts like a field hockey team. In the same time period, she also organized brass bands for the Irish Lesbian and Gay Organization (ILGO), where the ILGO band would play traditional Irish music while Irish queers were being arrested for trying to join the St. Patrick's Day Parade.

Reflecting on the impact of her performance training on this element of direct action, Jenny explained:

> I had learned all this stuff about having a brass band and how you organize it and the theatricality. . . . And also the fearlessness of just being on the street. Do theater anywhere. Go where people are, don't make them come to you, go where they are. You want to perform for people? Go where people are! And all this stuff about the carnivalesque providing this different kind of space in high stress situations with police.

Also in 1992, the same year the Lesbian Avengers formed, a feminist direct action group formed in New York out of outrage over the sexist travesty of Clarence Thomas's Supreme Court appointment. They set out a broad mission: economic parity and representation for all women; an end to homophobia, racism, religious prejudice and violence against women; and every woman's right to quality health care, childcare and reproductive freedom.

Jenny got involved in the Women's Action Coalition (WAC)'s drum corps, but WAC's culture was a shock—she was used to rank and file grassroots organizing, and WAC included wealthy women, connections with the moneyed part of the arts world, people who were coming to activism for the first time. She remembers asking someone to wait for a minute in a drum corps rehearsal and the woman threw a whistle at her face! She was appalled, explaining "I had been in the movement for twenty years and no one had *ever* thrown anything at my face in a meeting or rehearsal."

Still, WAC pulled off a number of powerful direct actions. The drum corps was flown to Houston for the 1992 Republican National Convention, where far-Right Presidential candidate Pat Buchanan would publicly declare a "culture war" against radical feminism, homosexuality, and abortion rights. Jenny remembers being in a thirty-woman drum corps, jumping out of an ice cream truck and performing all over Houston.

While this was a period of tremendous organizing, community-building, and visibility for queer and feminist communities, internal community debates defining who did or didn't belong were virulent. Jenny was painfully kicked out of the Lesbian Avengers when, for the first time, she became romantically involved with a man. She told the person kicking her out: "You're putting me in the closet! I've been a lesbian my entire life. Why on earth would you assume that I'm straight, which I'm not, and why would you assume that I'm not going to identify as a lesbian?"

Thankfully, there were some who didn't reject Jenny for the range of her queer desires. Through her involvement in the Lesbian Avengers, Jenny had joined a lesbian country western band called The Traveling Millies, singing and playing accordion along with fellow musicians and Avengers, Betsy Crenshaw and Harriet Hirschorn. Jenny proposed that the Traveling Millies do a version of "Bye Bye Love" changed to "Bi-Bi-Sexual." At first Harriet Hirschorn didn't want to, because she was committed to the band focusing on lesbian visibility. But by the next rehearsal, Harriet had changed her mind, telling Jenny, "Our consciousness has to grow! We have to do the song because you're real and you're reflecting the life of a lesbian."

Throughout 1992, while continuing her work closely with the Great Small Works collective and running around in various queer and feminist bands, Jenny was also in graduate school for Performance Studies at NYU. On the day of the Presidential election, November 3rd, she cast her vote and picked up a New York Post newspaper. On page two, she found a headline blaring: *AIDS VICTIM PROTESTS FROM BEYOND THE GRAVE.*

The article reported the political funeral of Mark Lowe Fisher, a member of an AIDS Coalition to Unleash Power (ACT UP) affinity group called "The Marys," one of many such sub-groups of ACT UP members that joined together to strategize and carry out direct actions, study groups, and other organizing.[33] The Marys are especially infamous for their powerful direct actions including an interruption of the MacNeil/Lehrer Report television news show and their "Stop the Church" action.

Mark Lowe Fisher had requested that his dead body be delivered to the Bush-Quayle campaign headquarters in Manhattan, writing "I want my own funeral to be fierce and defiant to make the public statement that my death from AIDS is a form of political assassination." His political funeral took place on the eve of Election Day, and only weeks after the ACT UP "Ashes Action" in which members dumped the ashes of their friends, lovers, and comrades on the lawn of the White House. Speakers at Fisher's funeral-demonstration made statements explaining that they were placing his body and the blame for his death at the doorstep of George H. W. Bush, "the man who murdered him," warning that they would turn the (first) Bush White House into a "symbolic graveyard of our dead."[34]

Jenny went on to write her masters thesis on ACT UP's use of political funerals. Interviewing members of The Marys, she learned that

33   http://www.actupny.org/documents/CDdocuments/Affinity.html.
34   Jenny Romaine. "Political Funerals in the Context of the AIDS Crisis" (MA thesis, New York University, 1993). I refer to excerpts selected for a CHAMP Forum I attended on May 13, 2009. For more about The Marys see also: https://hemi.nyu.edu/hemi/en/e-misferica-61/levine; http://www.actupny.org/diva/polfunsyn.html.

Mark Lowe Fisher had seen an article in the *John James AIDS Treatment Newsletter* that highlighted the history of political funerals in a number of other countries. The Marys researched the logistics of this kind of action and also discussed their wishes for their own funerals. Did they want "something solemn and symbolic" or something angry, like "having your body made into a funeral pyre and pushed off towards the Statue of Liberty?"[35] People talked of having their bodies impaled on the White House fence, or "being dragged through the streets of New York City pulled by a horse," as Michael Marko (a member of The Marys) told Jenny, "wearing white jeans of course."

As a theater performer and scholar, Jenny witnessed and documented the impact of spectacle within these AIDS activist strategies. In conversations with Jenny twenty years after these actions, Michael Marko's quote stays with her,

> The idea of that kind of creativity—you know, "wearing white jeans." It just struck me as—only a gay person would say that. Or a really fabulous woman. Everything was about this resilience.

Jenny wasn't a regular at ACT UP meetings, but she showed up for many of the weekly Monday night meetings,[36] and participated in a number of civil disobedience actions. She had a lot of friends involved in ACT UP, and she was "blown away" by the courage she witnessed, and the lessons about "death and about taboo and transgression and about being effective politically." She remembers watching journalist and ACT UP activist Esther Kaplan being dragged out of public meetings by cops, always "taking a lot of furniture with her" as she held onto chairs and table legs while being pulled away. Jenny reflected that she was drawn to document ACT UP's political funerals for multiple reasons. In addition to being personally impacted by the AIDS crisis, she was a political street theater maker and performer, and she saw a relationship

---

35   Quoting James Bagget in Jenny Romaine's thesis.
36   ACT UP New York's General Meeting still meets (25 years later) on Mondays, 7:30PM at the LGBT Center, 208 West 13th Street in Manhattan.

between the strategies and methodologies of theater and direct action protest. In her thesis, Jenny explored the theatrical question[37] "What is it that makes you want to look?"

> What are the points of expressive power one finds, or unlocks, through the placement of bodies in time and space? What makes the eye settle on a performer, the audience come closer, or an image have a life beyond the moment of its presentation? In activism one seems to be looking for similar openings. On what sites or social stages can relationships of power be made tangible, or revised? Both theater and activism seem to generate focus where it did not previously exist."[38]

ACT UP activist Jon Greenberg, who died in 1993, also described the theatrical power of ACT UP and their methodology of generating focus by "staging" performative actions beyond "the bounds of the physical theatrical space."

They are theatre in the world, and accomplish the types of reactions, actions, and catharsis that all people in the "conventional theatre" only dream about. We use the same tools, however. Research, intensive pre-production planning, bringing together the actors (demonstrators), rehearsing them and getting to their motivating emotions (anger, fear, loss, love for each other), sets, props, fundraising, publicity—all this for the single goal of creating a spectacle that will change people's lives and change the world (beyond shame.)[39]

---

37   In her thesis, Jenny refers to Esther Kaplan's article "Political Funeral." http://www.movementresearch.org/criticalcorrespondence/blog/?p=1082.
38   Jenny Romaine. "Political Funerals in the Context of the AIDS Crisis."
39   In Patrick Moore, *Beyond Shame: Reclaiming the Abandoned History of Radical Gay Sexuality*, 139.

A MONTAGE THEORY OF MAKING CULTURE

Jenny describes herself as a *chosid* of Dr. Barbara Kirshenblatt-Gimblett—the term for a devotee of a Hasidic rabbi. Truly, this teacher has had a tremendous influence on Jenny's life and work.

In 1983, as an undergrad at NYU, Jenny won an essay contest to be one of a student group traveling internationally with Kirshenblatt-Gimblett (who Jenny often refers to as BKG) for the whole school year. This honors program focused on the study of tourist performance as folklore, and the relationship between ritual and tourist performance, often through immersion in festivals. The program traveled to Japan, Bali, India, Kenya, Egypt, and Israel—an astounding opportunity, and Jenny's first time out of the US. In addition to studying the folklore of each culture they visited, and practicing their anthropology skill sets, Jenny and the other members of the program were on a major learning curve about colonial history, orientalism, neo-liberalism, and neo-colonial critique.

Jenny was horrified by witnessing the occupation of Palestine. Growing up in Yiddish Leftist culture, she hadn't been exposed to much Israel-oriented Jewish culture or Zionist politics. After her travels, back in New York, Jenny wrote her undergrad thesis about the politics of tourist performance in Jerusalem. Her work was critically anti-occupation, and she presented it decked out in a colonial outfit: jodhpurs and a pith helmet.

In 1986, Dr. Kirshenblatt-Gimblett connected Jenny with a job at the YIVO Center for Jewish Research. Jenny went on to work in the YIVO sound archives for the next thirteen years. There, using her folklore training from BKG and her "native listener" Yiddish skills, she conducted oral history interviews and catalogued records, radio broadcasts, and other sound materials.

YIVO (*Yidisher Visnshaftlekher Institut*) was founded in 1925 by scholars in Vilnius[40] and Berlin with the mission of documenting the Yiddish culture of Eastern Europe. YIVO came out of an interwar movement that talked about *doikayt*—hereness—a commitment to Jewish survival where they were (Eastern Europe), as opposed to many who were leaving with the (pre-State) Zionist movement or the promise of a better life in America. The YIVO archive project was a response to big questions about how to build an economically viable life in Europe, how to build a sense of possibility despite being brutally oppressed at a structural level. YIVO theorist Max Weinreich talked about *der veg tsu undzer yugnt*—"the way to our youth," how to empower "people in the process of becoming" to become something where they lived.

Jenny explains that the Jews of Eastern Europe knew that the rich folklore—melodies, practices, stories passed by word of mouth—were important to document.

> They saw that on the power side of the equation, Jews had this amazing culture. . . . Every melody, every *kehila* [community], every newspaper, every traditional practice was on the plus side of their power economy.

---

40   At the time, Vilnius was part of Poland; now it's in Lithuania.

> They went out to all the *shtetlach*, and they *zogt* [said] "sing me every melody you know," and they recorded it. They went and they took all the record books from the Jewish communities. These [archivists] were Socialists, but they saw that in every aspect of religious life and traditional life—in the foodways and you name it—there is information to be transmitted and that this was a cultural powerbank. And they wanted to develop it, and they said that it's going be through the rearrangement of these fragments, that we create something new.[41]

In the language of today's movement building, YIVO created an asset-based organizing campaign—the strategy of starting with recognition of what you already have in abundance, and using those strengths to build power. During the interwar period, academics and amateur *zamlers* (collectors) eagerly gathered documentation of books, artifacts, jokes, folktales, songs—the folk-life of European Jewry—and all of these were classified and recorded.[42]

In 1941, the Nazis occupied Vilnius and killed most of the YIVO community, transferring some of the archive collection to a center for the documentation of Jewish extinction, and destroying the rest. A group of Jews assigned to sort the Nazi collection, "the Paper Brigade," defiantly hid what they could in secret locations in the Vilne[43] ghetto.[44] After WWII, a few surviving members of the Paper Brigade returned, and there was a dedicated effort by survivors and researchers to reclaim archival documents that had been hidden away by resistance groups like the Paper Brigade in Vilnius and the Oyneg Shabbes group in Warsaw.[45] After the fall of the Nazis, the materials that were saved were

---

41   "Jenny Romaine on Shtetl."

42   See Itzik Nakhmen Gottesman's *Defining the Yiddish Nation: The Jewish Folklorists of Poland*, and Gabriella Safran's *Wandering Soul: The Dybbuk's Creator, S. An-sky*.

43   Vilnius in Yiddish is Vilne/Vilna.

44   That these materials exist and survived to reach New York is nothing short of miraculous, and has been well documented in David E. Fishman's *The Rise of Modern Yiddish Culture*.

45   An archive that was created by a secret team in the Warsaw Ghetto, led by historian Emmanuel Ringelblum. For more information, see Samuel D. Kassow's *Who Will Write Our History?: Rediscovering a Hidden Archive from the Warsaw Ghetto*.

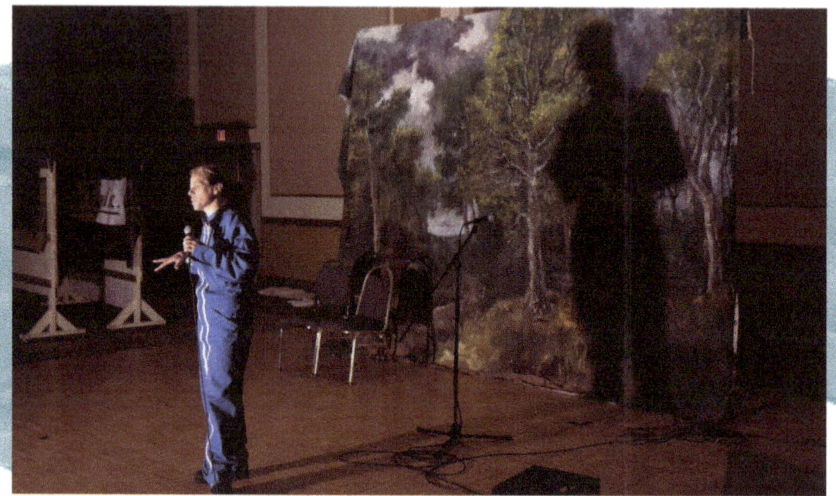

Jenny Romaine, KlezKamp Youth Theater Workshop 2008 (Photo credit: Alan Lankin)

once again endangered and partially destroyed under Stalinism. Another underground rescue mission arose to spirit what could be carried out to America. While only a fraction of the massive original collection was saved, it was a basis for re-building a major archive in NYC. Today, the YIVO collection holds over twenty-three million items, including books, documents, recordings, photographs, and other artifacts.[46]

Jenny worked at YIVO with a diverse group of colleagues. It was her first experience of Yiddish culture as a "big tent" that could include European native-Yiddish-speakers, Hasids, Bundists, people working together intergenerationally, men and women, queer and straight . . . she felt the unifying power of their commitment to valuing the lives archived in the YIVO collection. Through the archival materials, they were in "lively dialogue" with each other and with the dead.[47]

She worked intimately with the sound archive of Yiddish European life, including a major shipment of newly discovered materials that had been hidden in Vilnius. Jenny remembers that when they opened these box-

46   "YIVO Institute for Jewish Research | About YIVO." YIVO Institute for Jewish Research. https://www.yivo.org/About-YIVO.
47   Interview by Pauline Katz.

es, everyone wept with the weight of recognition that the people who had created and contributed to the archives were almost all gone, and the materials represented the everyday lives of communities lost to genocide.[48] It was in this work that she started to develop a sense of the importance of fragments.

The ethnographic archive of Eastern European Jewry is fragmented due to a legacy of repression, oppression, and genocide. The fragments that the YIVO researchers and the many volunteer collectors gathered amidst anti-Jewish policies and pogroms, and then what survived the destruction of Nazism and Stalinism, are what remains of the "cultural powerbank." Jenny was working intimately with these fragments of our cultural legacy, and she came to see that she could work with these pieces through her artistic practice—rearranging, layering, and montaging them—remixing history to build new culture.[49]

> I experienced the vibrancy of [interwar Yiddish] culture and its political and religious diversity in full living color. So I don't have a nostalgic feeling about it. It feels very real to me, and I feel blessed by that. It's not like "ohhh, my *bubbe's kuklefl!*" My grandmother's cooking spoon!" It's more like "who were the avant-garde Yiddish puppeteers in Vilne, and what were they dealing with artistically and formally?" I feel very connected to that montage theory of history, and that is how I make art.[50]

It is this methodology that Jenny describes as "ethnographic surrealism," borrowing a term from a concept explored by James Clifford in his book *The Predicament of Culture: Twentieth-Century Ethnography, Literature and Art.* This concept acknowledges that researchers can and indeed always do play a role as artist, curator, and designer of gathered cultural fragments and their interpreted meanings. Clifford describes

---

48   "Jenny Romaine on Shtetl."
49   Ibid.
50   Ibid.

ethnography as "an explicit form of cultural critique sharing radical perspectives with Dada and surrealism"[51] and elaborates:

> The surrealist elements of modern ethnography tend to go unacknowledged by a science that sees itself engaged in the reduction of incongruities rather than, simultaneously, in their production. But is not every ethnographer something of a surrealist, a reinventor and reshuffler of realities? … Surrealism coupled with ethnography recovers its early vocation as critical cultural politics.[52]

I also see this work as very aligned with Gloria Anzaldúa's writing about "autohistoria," which she describes as a methodology of "rereading and rewriting" cultural histories as a strategy to "expose the limitations in the existing paradigms and create new stories of healing, self-growth, cultural critique, and individual/collective transformation."[53]

NEW YIDDISH THEATER

In 1994, Jenny's YIVO colleagues Adrienne Cooper and Henry "Hank" Sapoznik co-founded KlezKamp: The Yiddish Folk Arts Program,[54] which went on to run for thirty years as an annual five-day gathering held during Christmas week in a "Borscht Belt" Jewish retreat center in the Catskills region of Upstate New York. A forum for intergenerational learning and celebration within Yiddish folk culture, the gathering included classes and performances focused on Yiddish dance, music, language, storytelling, visual arts, food, and more. A few years into

---

51   Clifford, *The Predicament of Culture*, 12.

52   Ibid.,147.

53   Gloria Anzaldúa and AnaLouise Keating. *The Gloria Anzaldúa Reader* (Durham: Duke University Press, 2009), 319.

54   "About Us." *Living Traditions: Community-Based Yiddish Folk Culture.* http://www.living-traditions.org/docs/about.htm.

the gathering, Jenny saw that there was no programming for teens and adolescents, so she invented the KlezKamp Youth Theater Workshop, which functioned as a key laboratory for developing her craft in community with Yiddish arts colleagues.

The history of Yiddish American theater is often told through the tension between high art shows intended to be serious educational drama and the cheap "*shund*" ("trash") entertainment shows. There were also multiple schools of experimental, avant-garde, political Yiddish theater—including Surrealist, Constructivist, Expressionist, Suprematist, and Futurist movements. And there were radical Yiddish puppeteers such as Modicut, the company of Zuni Maud and Yosl Cutler.

The Youth Theater Workshop created an opportunity for Jenny to develop a methodology of making "New Yiddish Theater." More specifically, she devised a way of producing Yiddish avant-garde folk art with content drawn from the YIVO archives, borrowing methods from the legacies of experimental Yiddish arts, the *zamler* (amateur collector) ethnography traditions, and radical politics in Yiddish culture. And doing so with intergenerational creative collaborators.

> How do you deal with the chasm [between Yiddish speaking generations and the youth]? You jump across it, *you are the bridge.* You learn and you develop and you do fieldwork (which is a YIVO thing). You collect, you collect, you collect—while the people are around — and you learn from each other.[55]

Jenny explains that New Yiddish Theater braids multiple elements together, but we should always be able to distinguish each element of the show. What is the *new* piece, or the modern cultural information? What is the *Yiddish* piece, the cultural/historical/archival fragments? What is the *theater* piece, the craft, or framing element? And one more cru-

---

55   Interview by Pauline Katz.

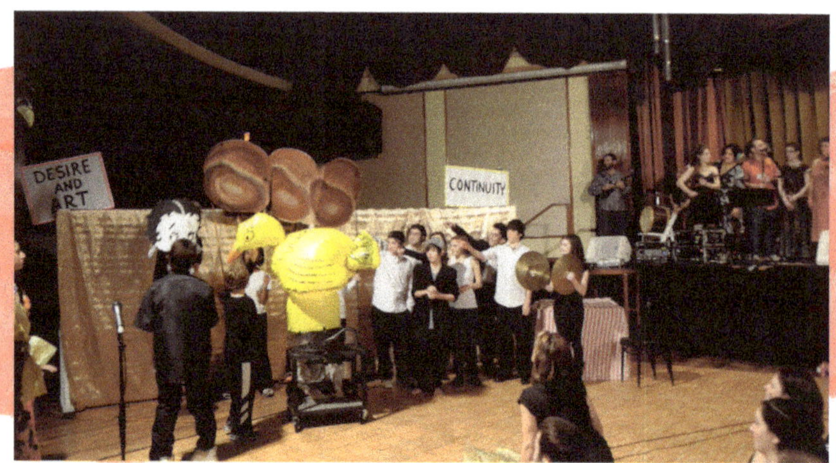

KlezKamp Youth Theater Workshop 2009 (Photo credit: Alan Lankin)

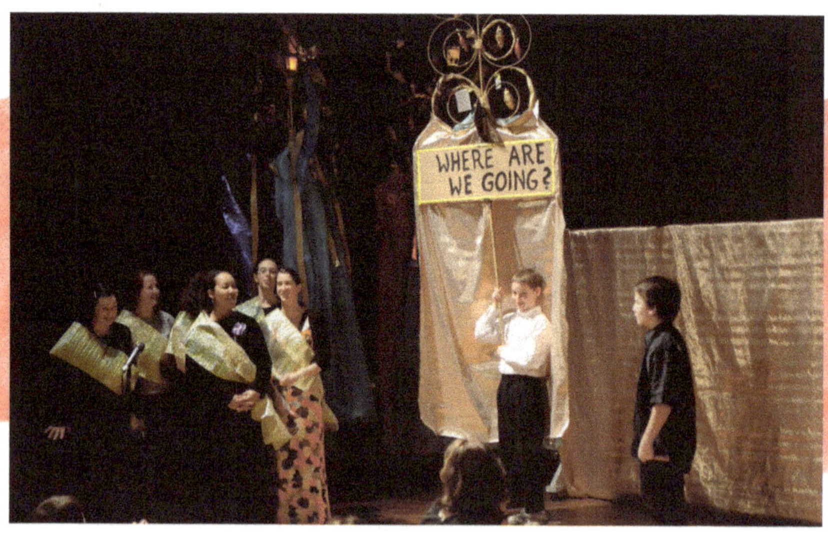

KlezKamp Youth Theater Workshop 2009 (Photo credit: Alan Lankin)

cial piece always braided in: what are the *politics*, the issue, what's at stake?[56]

In a show built for the 13th anniversary of KlezKamp and the 100th anniversary of the Yiddisher Arbeiter Bund (Jewish Labor Party), the Youth Theater Workshop participants did ethnographies of all of the youth's bar/bat mitzvahs and also studied the Bund documentary film *Mir Kumen* and Yiddish play *Hirshl Leckert,* about a revolutionary youth martyr. The show put these content pieces into dialogue with each other. "Our piece was so good," says Jenny, "it was so dialectical."

> We were looking at the Bund, we were thinking about ourselves, and then at the end it was that thing where you put the fragments together and all the sudden you feel something really big, but you wouldn't get there unless you started doing that layering.[57]

This part of our interview was emotional for Jenny—she explained that she wasn't sad, she was happy to be able to honor her family's history with this show about Jewish revolutionary organizing. Not just telling a story about them, but teaching young people what revolutionary energy *feels like*—the same thing Jenny learned from her family who had "seen the tipping point happen" and knew that social transformation was possible. She is teaching young people to prepare for revolutionary moments, embedding resistance strategies in her theater methodology. As she learned from her family: you don't just dream about it, or ask God to save you—you make it happen through organizing, applying pressure, collectively. Jenny is using theater to teach about being a revolutionary through rehearsing resistance.

> The Youth Theater Workshop was a space for great experimentation, and they never shut it down. . . . In a lot of other "Jewish environments," because they don't acknowledge the existence

---

56   Mattson, "What Can Jewish Be?"
57   Interview by Pauline Katz.

> of worker's movements or revolutionary thought, they repress
> it and they shut you out and they shut you down, or they kick you
> out. But in KlezKamp there was always this thing that we totally
> respect the religious people and we totally respect the queers
> and we totally respect the Left people and everyone in between,
> and it's a big tent. They fought hard for that, and they made that
> community. So my doing Yiddish theater work really came out of
> KlezKamp.[58]

Jenny credits KlezKamp as the place she found her artistic voice. While her methods have deep connections to the history of avant-garde Yiddish theater, they are equally influenced by her contemporary artists in the field of modern Yiddish music, many of whom have been friends and colleagues connected through KlezKamp.

Jenny's close friendship and creative collaboration with Yiddish singer, activist, and scholar Adrienne Cooper (*zts"l* [59]) is a crucial part of this story. Cooper was assistant director at the YIVO Institute for Jewish Research while Jenny worked there, and went on to become the Executive Officer for Programming and then Executive Officer for External Affairs for the (Yiddish organization) Workmen's Circle/Arbeter Ring. With Adrienne's untimely death in 2011, at 65 years old, Yiddishland lost a cultural powerhouse and a beloved leader. At Adrienne's memorial service, Jenny re-read text from her presentation of the 2010 Marshall T. Meyers Risk Taker Award from Jews for Racial and Economic Justice.

> Adrienne's movement is a political work of art in which every
> fragment of what folk do can be used to chart a new political
> course. . . . Adrienne Cooper is a fearless guide . . . who has made
> sure that no one is excluded from this resource and no power
> can silence it. She brings people, ideas, and buildings together to

---

58   Ibid.
59   Jewish honorific for the dead; "May the memory of the righteous be a blessing." Adrienne Cooper died on December 25, 2011.

> create spaces for unimaginable political joy and artistic joy. She is a forest of Jewish sound, a joyous crowd, a resistance fighter, a lover, I would add: a flirt, a screaming rhetorical street poster and a *tzaddik*. For all of this [she receives this award], and for never working from a place of choseness or nostalgia, but from a place of justice and empathy and complex Yiddish polyphony.[60]

Members of The Klezmatics are also key creative partners and contemporaries for Jenny. Founded in 1986, Grammy-winning band The Klezmatics are tributed with a key role in Klezmer's modern revival. Like Jenny, The Klezmatics insist on a non-nostalgic relationship with the historical content and form, saying "We want to make sure that we are part of a living tradition, and living traditions change; they don't stay in a pickled form."[61] Their music and lyrics aren't only a memorial of Yiddish-past, they're talking about their lives in the present. Witness their 1988 album *Shvaygn = Toyt* (Silence = Death), which band member Frank London explains was "both an homage to the slogan of ACT UP, and an acknowledgment that if one is silent in the face of injustice then one is siding with the oppressor. It was also a literal statement about the Yiddish language: if no one speaks or sings in it, it will be dead."[62] London adds:

> By putting forth a consistent and coherent political and aesthetic Yiddish/klezmer music that embraces our political values—supporting gay rights, workers' rights, human rights, universal religious and spiritual values expressed through particular art forms—and eschewing the aspects of Yiddish/Jewish culture that are nostalgic, tacky, kitschy, nationalistic and misogynistic, we have shown a way for people to embrace Yiddish culture on their own terms as a living, breathing part of our world and its political and aesthetic landscape.

---

60 "Some Excerpts from the Memorial Service for Adrienne Cooper." Jewish Currents.
61 "Bio." Klezmer Music from The Klezmatics, New York Klezmer Band. Accessed April 28, 2013. http://klezmatics.com/about/bio.
62 Ibid, http://klezmatics.com/about/bio/expanded-bio/4.

When Jenny layers archival content with modern/pop culture content, she often talks about this as "sampling"—referencing the hip-hop practice of taking pieces of other songs and mixing them into new beats. Jenny expresses a feeling of kinship with the work of Montreal musician Josh Dolgin, aka SoCalled, a fellow KlezKamp teacher and rapper/producer who mixes samples from the YIVO sound archive into his music with humor and wit, as in his albums *HiphopKhasene* (2003), *The So Called Seder: A Hip-Hop Haggadah* (2005) and *Ghettoblaster* (2007). Ethnomusicologist Shayn Smulyan writes about SoCalled's use of sampling Yiddish content and identifies it as part of a trend toward fusion and reinterpretation in contemporary Yiddish music[63]

KlezKamp also created a new generation of talented, informed, political adults who are emerging artists and folk-culture creators, fluent in *Yiddishkeit* (Yiddish culture) if not the language itself. After three decades, many of the teens from the early years of the program have become a creative community of musicians and performers that work with Jenny on many productions.

The band Yiddish Princess (YP) is one example of this trend, made up of people who grew up in the KlezKamp Youth Theater Workshop and/or work with Jenny as musical partners in projects including the Sukkos Mob and the Afselakhis Spectacle Committee's Purim-productions. Yiddish Princess performs classic Yiddish poems and songs in heavy metal and modern rock versions. YP is far from shtick or nostalgia, as these musicians are active members of the vibrant evolving Yiddish arts and culture movement based in New York City. Singer Sarah Gordon grew up attending KlezKamp as the daughter of founder Adrienne Cooper. She participates in Yiddish as a vernacular culture and as a member of the often post-vernacular Yiddish music scene. Yiddish Princess answers to a commentary that Alicia Svigal, an early member of the Klezmatics, offers: if not for the cultural destruction of the Holocaust,

63   Shayn E Smulyan, "The SoCalled Past: Sampling Yiddish in Hip-Hop," from Choosing Yiddish: New Frontiers of Language and Culture (Detroit: Wayne State University Press, 2012) 357-376.

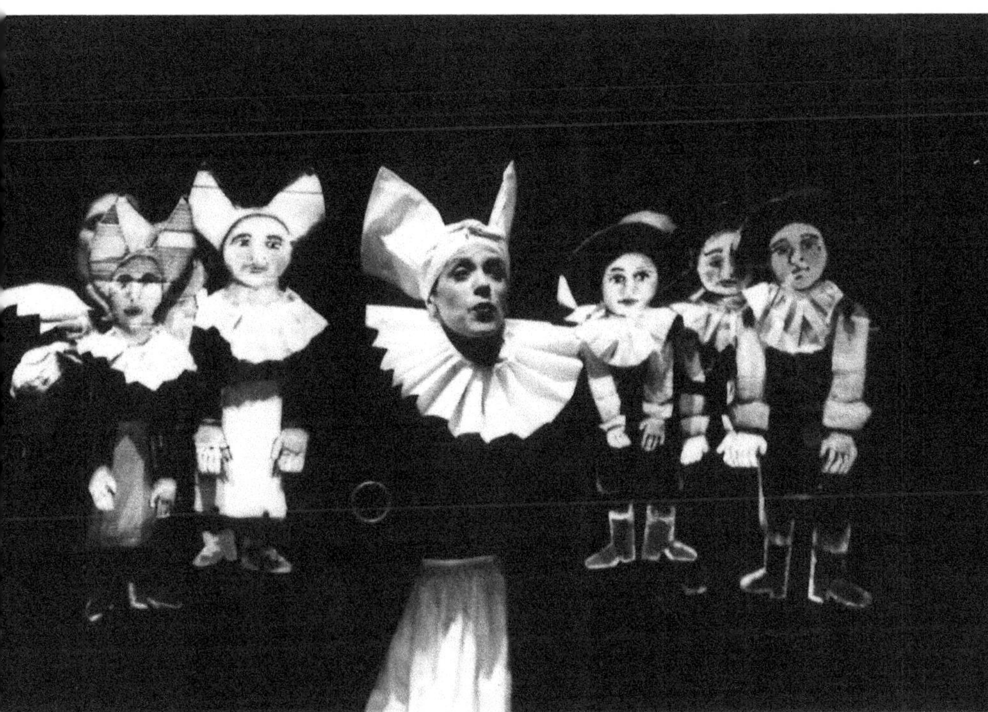

Glückel of Hameln, 1999 (Photo credit: Richard Termine)

"there would be Yiddish rock bands today, playing the kind of music we play."[64] This is a fabulous example of Yiddish culture that goes beyond nostalgia into the process of regeneration.

During KlezKamp's first decade, another major creative production evolved out of Jenny's relationships at YIVO—the show *Glückel of Hameln*, produced and performed throughout 1999 and 2000. Jewish feminist organization Ma'ayan commissioned Jenny and Adrienne Cooper to make this show about historical figure Glückel of Hameln, in connection with a series of posters for Women's History Month. The title character was the first woman to write her memoir in Yiddish, in 1690 C.E. Married at fourteen, by the age of forty-four Glückel was a widow with twelve children. She became a successful businesswoman while navigating and documenting life in Germany amidst virulent anti-Semitism. Jenny recalls:

---

64   Shandler. Adventures in Yiddishland, 144.

> It's hysterical, she's like a *maggid* [storyteller]. She tells you all these sexy parables to make you pay attention. She's telling you how sad she is, and she puts in all these spicy stories. She's living in a world where she's a totally marginalized outsider. . . . They can't own land, they have no rights. She's writing from inside this totally marginalized position and she has to hold fast to her values. The whole world thinks she's the devil. The more I read about it, the more I realized, you know, she's passing these engraved stone bridges with pictures of Jews sucking shit out of the ass of a pig and being led by Satan. So the level of antagonism this person is existing within . . . it's intense! And yet she writes these stories about how they maintained their life.[65]

The stories reminded Jenny of a theatrical form called *bånklsang*, bench-singing, which she had learned from Bread and Puppet. A form of "literature for the illiterate" that was performed in the marketplace in Glückel's time, a *bånklsang* was a sung-ballad narrating images on giant paintings that riled people up to buy illustrated broadsheets of the lurid tales after the performance.

Jenny and Adrienne Cooper collaborated with The Klezmatics' Frank London to create ballads based on Glückel's memoirs, and they built a show with a spectacular group of artists and performers. The content was a rich source for exploring class, money and the marketplace, anti-Semitism, feminism, and what it means to stick to your values. Glückel's children were portrayed by puppets, and she herself was portrayed by two people in a shared costume because "she was so much woman that it took two people to womanifest her!"[66] The show was performed in a mixture of Yiddish and English.

---

65 Ibid.
66 Ibid.

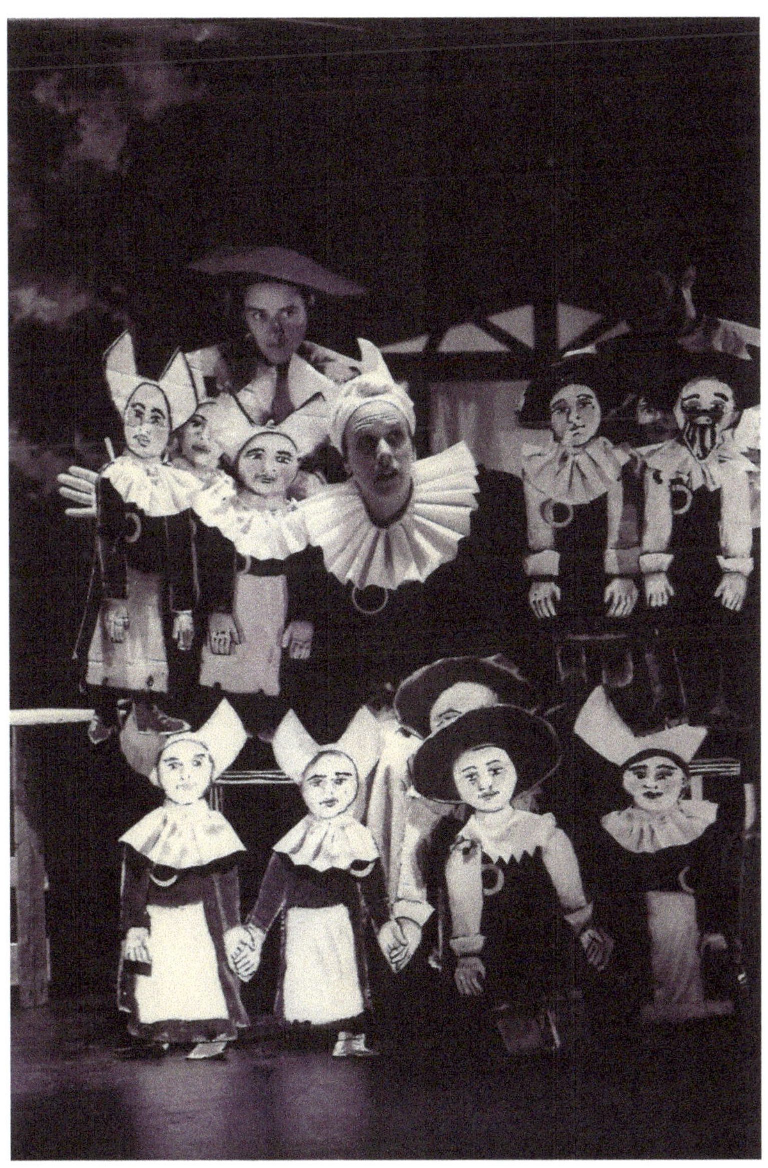

Glückel of Hameln, 1999 (Photo credit: Richard Termine)

Playbill described the memoirs as "part Talmudic interpretation, part news flash, part economic theory and part medieval Jewish legend."[67] The *New York Times* theater review called the show an "unusual and highly creative excursion into autobiography, history, music, art, and language."[68] The production toured around the country and abroad, playing to packed-house audiences that ran the spectrum from Orthodox feminists to radical Leftists. In New York, the show played for over two weeks at the La Mama ETC space in January and February of 2000.

In a *Village Voice* interview that year with Alisa Solomon, the co-creators reflected on their use of Yiddish in the show and their commitment to Yiddish culture as a living thing. Adrienne Cooper explained: "This is Yiddish theater as it should be: in dialogue with contemporary culture and not seeing itself in continuous retrospective." "We're not naïve," adds Frank London, "We aren't saying Yiddish is going to return as the living language it was 100 years ago. But you can't deny that it's infusing the music, poetry, and theater of today's American-Ashkenazi Jews." The last line in the interview is Cooper's: "We have a deep love and respect and passion for Yiddish culture. What we don't have is nostalgia."[69]

In 1996, a second annual Yiddishland forum was established: KlezKanada. Held each summer since then in the Laurentian mountain region just north of Montreal, KlezKanada presented Jenny another space to practice New Yiddish Theater in community. At KlezKanada, the performances are intergenerational (as opposed to KlezKamp's Youth Theater Workshop) and with the warm weather, Jenny can build giant spectacles using the landscape, as Bread & Puppet does in Vermont.

The first time Jenny worked at KlezKanada, she had recently heard Yiddishist Michael Wex kvetching that parades at Yiddish gatherings

---

67   Christine Ehren, "La MaMa Gluckel of Hameln Adds Two Performances Feb. 12 & 13." *Playbill*.
68   Lawrence Van Gelder, "Theater Review: Motherly Advice in Yiddish With Historical Asides," *The New York Times*, February 1, 2000.
69   Alisa Solomon, "A Yiddishe Mama Courage," *Village Voice*, January 18, 2000.

tended to replicate "*goyish* Mardi Gras" style instead of drawing from Yiddish culture. This prompted her to research Yiddish processional examples, including a conversation with Itzik Gottesman, friend and former YIVO colleague, who has been a major content provider for Jenny's work. Gottesman shared a story he had heard from a man named Aryeh Leish whose village in Stanashest, Rumania had a 1920s tradition of gathering to greet the Sabbath at a body of water, and then singing a melody and playing their instruments, marching backwards into town.

So, on the Friday night of KlezKanada that year, the attendees explored a world built by Jenny and the members of her workshop, going on a collective woodland tour through case studies of how Jews walk together, including a recreation of a *shabbes shpatzir*—where girls would walk and sing to each other in a competition for the saddest ballads. The tour took them past DJ Reena Katz spinning ambient beats on her turntable; elders performing Hasidic songs while sitting on big rocks with bows and arrows; and finally to Dr. Barbara Kirshenblatt-Gimblett performing as YIVO founder Max Weinreich, talking about his youth movement *Di Biener*, backed up by a big brass band. All of this led the audience to a lakeside waterfront to kick off a backwards processional to greet the Sabbath. Jenny had taught the song to each instrumental group separately so that when they joined together at the water, they all heard the whole song for the first time together.

> It was so deep. It was a real case study. It was in the landscape. It was four hundred people. They were blown away. And now they do it every year, it's a tradition at the camp. To me it's so anti-militarist, it's so Dada that in the 1920s they would be like "we're not marching in your fascist lines. We're not marching in your fascist armies, we're walking backwards."

In 2014, a couple of years after hearing about it from Jenny, I finally experienced the backwards marching shabbes ritual for myself. The gathering started with a moment of silence for a beloved violin teacher

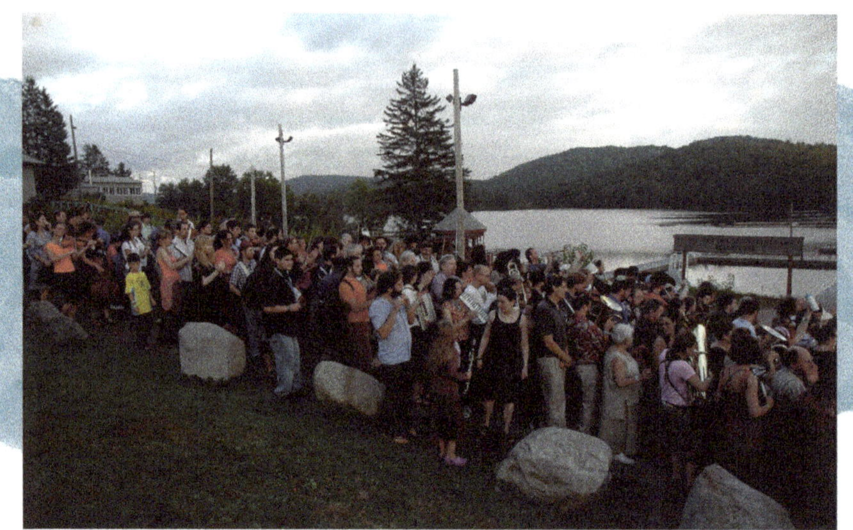

KlezKanada backwards march, 2007. (Photo credit: Alan Lankin)

who had passed away, then only the violins shared the first notes of the music—sounding out heart-pulling notes in honor of their teacher. In a swelling moment, the other instruments joined in, and the backward march began. What I hadn't known to expect, and what lifted me in a surprising emotional rush, was the way that the tune changed as I marched. As my pace brought me through different groups of instrumentalists, the repeating phrases of the song were new and chaotic and unpredictable even while repeating one traditional melody. By accessing the disorientation of walking backwards, these skilled and practiced musicians were performing in the collage-style of Jenny's theatrical productions. As we reached the top of the hill, I laughed out loud at a few instrumentalists playing us in from the roof of the dining hall. In the rare place where a fiddler on the roof isn't the requisite access point to Ashkenazi Jewish culture, we can still appreciate the joke.

In summer 2011, the KlezKanada theme was "Humor." Jenny knew right away that she wanted to make a ton of chicken puppets that walk through the landscape, because she also needed chickens for another project and she thinks they are a very Jewish bird. She also wanted to focus on a woman, because "there are so many women that are invisible to us." But she didn't want to talk about Sophie Tucker or anyone well-known, explaining that "the gift is to shine light on what we don't know." Itzik Gottesman provided the inspiration again, telling Jenny about a woman named Nekhame Epshteyn, a YIVO researcher who he had written about in his book on the Yiddish folklorists of Poland. Epshteyn had collected and catalogued over a thousand Yiddish jokes.[70]

> I was like *what?* Of course we're gonna make it all about this YIVO *aspirant* [scholar/grad student]. Because I'm totally interested in promoting the Weinreich model as a canon, as a way to be Jewish. Which is: you don't have to be a religious figure, and you don't have to be connected to Israel. It's a secular body of work.

Nekhame Epshteyn was a poet, translator, and teacher in the secular Yiddish schools in Vilne, and a key member of the YIVO Ethnographic Folklore Commission. Focused on humor, Epshteyn classified the jokes in her collection by both their "garb, the environment around the persons" and their "goal, what were they really laughing at."[71] Epshteyn escaped from the Vilne ghetto when the Germans occupied Lithuania, but was caught and killed in the 1942 Ponar massacre.

And so the Nekhame Epshteyn Chicken Park was born, using an amusement park run by chickens as a frame to teach about Nekhame Epshteyn and her Yiddish jokes. "The things that I have pulled off are *insane!*," says Jenny. "You built *what? A portable amusement park based on Yiddish ethnography?*"

Jenny dug into the Epshteyn files in the YIVO archive to learn a bunch of jokes. At the same time, she partnered with puppet engineer Sara Peat-

---

70   Thank you to Itzik Gottesman for this source: "In her article 'Vi azoy tsu klasifitsirn dem yidishn vits' [How to classify the Yiddish/Jewish joke] Nekhame Epstein writes that there were 100,000 items in the YIVO folklore collection, almost 63,000 had been inventoried. Her article is based on the 1,297 jokes that had been inventoried [leaving out the obscene ones]." YIVO-bleter, volume 12 and volumes 4-5, November - December, 1937: 484-493.
71   Itzik Nakhmen Gottesman. *Defining the Yiddish Nation: The Jewish Folklorists of Poland* (Detroit: Wayne State University Press, 2003), 159.

tie and brought in a bunch of volunteers to prep for the summer gathering, and together they created fifteen flat chickens, eight intricate life-sized marionette chickens, all the enclosures for the amusement park areas, and a giant chicken puppet—fifteen feet tall—to scare everyone at the end of the show. That summer, the crowd at KlezKanada toured a theme park built with hay bales and cardboard, decorated with Yiddish clairvoyant posters and newspaper articles.

At a bar, the chickens told jokes about drinking. At a cemetery, chickens told cemetery jokes. You could go to a clairvoyant chicken. You could meet Nekhame Epshteyn herself (chicken version) and tell her a joke of your own in her sound booth—if it was funny, a chicken would shoot out of a cannon. At a ticket booth, you could get your sins weighed and buy a ticket to the final night's show—*Truth in Gay Clothes: The Musar Musical.*

Jenny explained to the crowds that the Park was not manned, but run by chicken labor. There were some employment issues arising. Things were a little tense. It was foreshadowing: at *The Musar Musical,* the crowd would come to understand that the chickens were going on strike, just as in a story by classic Yiddish writer Sholem Aleichem, "No More Kapores, or The Sacrificial Chicken Revolt."

SURREALIST HOLIDAYS

Jenny grew up in a secular family that didn't go to synagogue and didn't observe Jewish holidays, but her family was informed about wider Jewish culture. Through her work in the YIVO archive, Jenny learned about Jewish religious life and started carrying a Jewish calendar to stay aware of what was going on in the ritual year. As a Yiddish culture-maker, she explains, the Jewish holiday-cycle is a rich source of content to engage throughout the year, "Very often people say, 'What should we do?' And I'm like 'what day of the month is it?' It's a wellspring of so much communal knowledge."

Purim is a favorite Jewish holiday for young people, feminists, queers, and party animals of all stripes. Purim's narrative, the Book of Esther (aka the *Megillah*), tells a tale of a foolish king, a woman refusing to dance naked for all the king's men, a beauty pageant, a secret revealed, and a time of tables-turning on the bad-guy known as Haman—*may his name be blotted out!* The springtime holiday calls for noisemaking, rule-breaking, blurring binaries, and an end to business as usual. All of those elements come together in a traditional folk play called a Purim-shpil, which has origins traced back as far as 1697.

Since 2002, Jews for Racial and Economic Justice (JFREJ) has sponsored a radical Purimshpil project founded by Adrienne Cooper and Jenny Romaine in partnership with the Workmen's Circle/Arbeter-Ring and the Great Small Works Theater Company. In the late 2000's, the Afselakhis Spectacle Committee[72] formed as a collective of artists and cultural producers who have continued to work with JFREJ and a long list of other artists and social justice organizations to produce Purim spectacles that bring together 500+ revelers each year for a wild time. This Purimshpil offers a powerful example of what can happen when we use our cultural abundance in our political organizing. The shows have enlivened, enlightened, confused, and inspired JFREJ members, comrades, and friends from 2002's *Giant Puppet Purim Ball Against the Death Penalty* to 2004's *Rehearsal for the Downfall of Shoeshine: An Immigrant Justice Purim Spectacular!* to 2007's *Roti and Homentaschn: The Palace Workers Revolt!* to 2013's *I See What You're Doing: Purim, Puppets, Politsey* and 2015's *Your Roots Are Showing: An Underground Purim Botanical.*[73]

---

72   *Afselakhis* is a Yiddish word meaning both "out of spite" and "in spite of."
73   The different spellings of *Homentaschn/en* reflect different transliterations from Yiddish and Hebrew.

Over the years, these radical Purimshpil events have helped JFREJ to strengthen and expand relationships with many artists and with allied organizations including CAAAV: Organizing Asian Communities, Communities United for Police Reform, Domestic Workers United, The HIV Prevention Justice Alliance, and Picture the Homeless.[74]

Working together to create these performances, singing together, rehearsing and building sets together, dancing together—it's the kind of relationship-building you just can't get in a meeting, or even at a demonstration. So many people keep coming back to participate in Purim because it's a rare time when we get to see our political partners as multidimensional people, coming from cultural strength and resourcefulness. It builds our power, to see ourselves and each other in that light.

On Purim, among other unusually encouraged activities, we are mandated to get so wasted that we can't tell the difference between our friends and our enemies. Some people drink, other people make surrealist theater that spins us round until we're not sure which end is up. Some people do both, as witnessed by the many years these early Purimshpils devolved into an all-night dance party without ever performing the final act.

Purim's topsy-turvy style is a great match for Jenny's surrealist aesthetics, but it's just one of many Jewish holidays that inspire her. Since 2005, Jenny has created and directed a semi-annual team of performers known as The Sukkos Mob, "an intergenerational company of spectacle singers, artists, and scholars who investigate the ancient autumnal harvest and pilgrimage holiday called Sukkos (or, in Hebrew, Sukkot) through a noisy and lyrical street spectacle."[75]

From an interview with JFREJ's *Beyond the Pale* radio show on WBAI:

---

74   Preceding three paragraphs written collaboratively by the author and Daniel Rosza Lang/Levitsky for the JFREJ website.
75   Press release from the author's personal email.

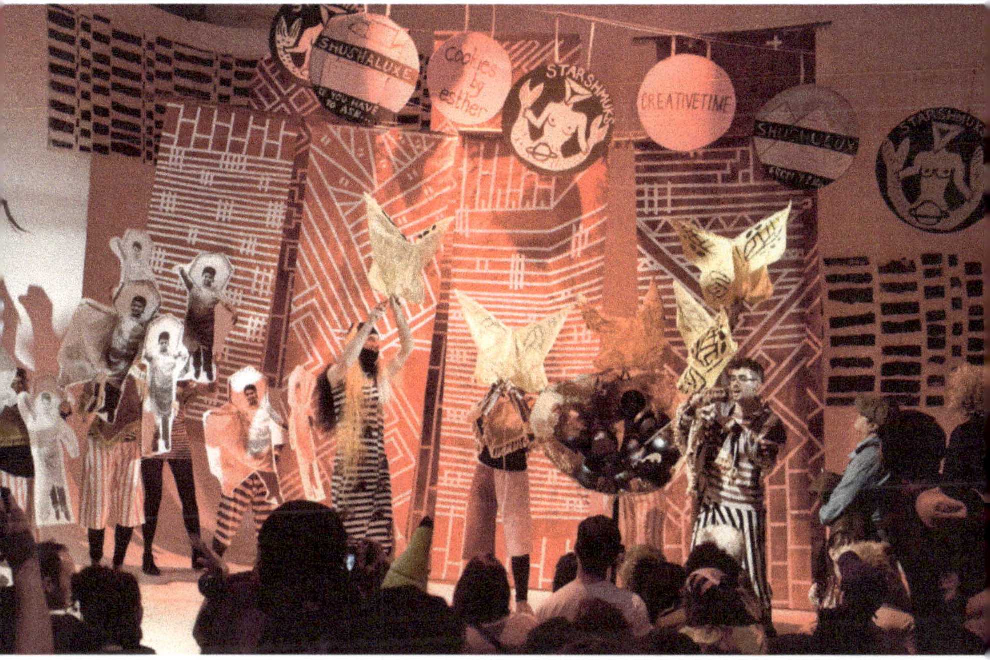

Purim 2014, "The Spawn of Estherlu Present Parthenogenesis: The Next Generation"
(Photo credit: Minister Erik McGregor)

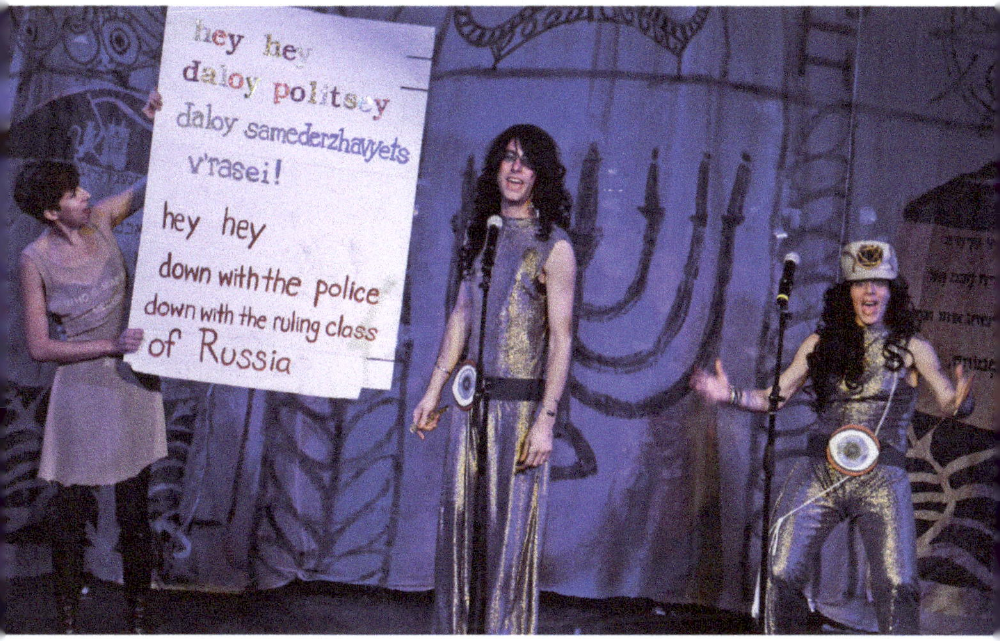

Purim 2013, "I See What You're Doing: Purim, Puppets, Politsey"
(Photo credit: Minister Erik McGregor)

I was riding around in these Hasidic neighborhoods, as I often do. You know, I speak the Yiddish language, I'm interested in it, and they are people who also speak that language and make art in that language so I consider them my co-artists in this Yiddish theater enterprise. What are they doing for Sukkos? I start reading all the posters. They're having a haunted house, they're having a festival, bungee jumping, the complete miniature recreation of the second temple, a monkey show. Separate shows for men and women. They're really doing it up. So I went to see some of these entertainments, and they're very carny [carnivalesque], and they're *awesome*. And I thought to myself, if they—as Yiddish theater makers—are *kibitzing* and delighting their people at this time, why should I not be doing the same?

Jenny recognized Sukkos as a holiday that is "undertouched" by secularists, compared to holidays like Passover and Purim, and so the Sukkos Mob was born. The Mobsters travel in a pack wearing uniforms loosely based on the yeshiva boy look but "a little more Sammy Davis, Junior. A little more Vegas"—meaning green suit jackets and white fedoras. Jenny explains, "I do think the yeshiva people look marvelous. But we don't copy any of their religious things, because of course they have value and it's never about mocking what people believe in. The interest in the project is to experience joy."[76]

The Sukkos Mob's motto is "FUN IS NOT JUST FOR FUNDAMENTALISTS!" In her interview with the Yiddish Book Center, Jenny responds to a question about her relationship with fundamentalism, shedding light on her decision to "throw her hat in the ring" of making Yiddish street theater in response to the Hasidic celebrations.

[Jewish fundamentalism is] very shocking to me because my tradition teaches me to be like: "Hey! I'm queer, you're Korean, she's queer and Korean! Let's play music!"... I think what a funda-

---

mentalist is, it's like it's gotta be talked about one way, and they try to make you feel like you have no right to be Jewish and be speaking as a Jew publicly, Jewishly. So I really had to interrogate that. I do think there are people who are religious and they work very hard to have what they have and I want to respect that and I don't want to be a cultural appropriator. I don't want to just mess with their traditions that they practice, and not respect the fact that they have deep and long histories related to them. But that doesn't mean that I don't want to investigate or talk about them, just as I would welcome them wanting to understand the traditions of the Left.

The shows are inspired by traditional celebratory Sukkos rituals—water libations, rain dance raves, torch dances, trumpet songs, juggling. Many of the shows are performed outside in public spaces in New York City– including Union Square and Times Square. Jenny adds that one reason for dressing up like Hasidim is that the cops are less likely to bust a religious group—we can point to the Chabadniks [traditionally dressed Hasidim] and say "Hey, we're just doing what they're doing!"

The Sukkos Mob performs at venues ranging from Times Square sidewalks to Yiddish day schools to Upper West Side synagogues, to a semi-weekly midtown event called Chulent which brings together a mix of Orthodox and Hasidic outsiders with random Jewish punks, anarchists, and assorted weirdos.[77]

The Sukkos Mob originated shortly after Hurricane Katrina hit New Orleans. Jenny heard performer and story-teller Amichai Lau-Lavie talking about the holiday's traditional rain dances and water libations, and that inspired her to use the traditions of Sukkos to address the aftermath of the hurricane and flood in New Orleans. In its first year of street theater performances, the Sukkos Mob called attention to the ongoing crisis in New Orleans using a beseeching classic cantorial song

---

77   Jennifer Bleyer,."City of Refuge,'" *The New York Times*, March 18, 2007.

for Sukkos, *Aneinu, Aneinu, Be Yom Koreinu,* which translates to "Answer Us, Answer Us, On the Day We Call."

The second year was about Iran, and Jewish-Iranian singer Galit Dardashdi taught the mobsters songs from her culture. Jenny explains:

> There was all this saber-rattling about bombing Iran. Iran is a great center of Jewish life, so we partnered with our Iranian Jewish friends, singing songs about rain in Farsi. We played in [Jewish] day schools, and we were role-modeling principled disobedience to Jewish kids, saying, "The Bush agenda is on, they won't let you protest the war, you've got this Homeland Security thing. It doesn't have to be this way, kids. You can think outside the box, you're allowed to think critically!" We would go in there as this mob of adults and do these amazingly beautiful, marvelously scored, weird shows that just left everybody feeling extremely— probably confused, but also very free. We were demonstrating that to celebrate Jewishly could include this kind of analysis. That theater is a great place to gestate ideas about domestic and foreign policy, while you sing the most beautiful song you've got in your repertoire, with the song led by a woman, and she is killin' it![78]

Another year, the show was called *Awesome is Over*—described by Jenny as "an ethnographically surreal tour of the senses" which she explained as a desire to be done with hating people and instead build a campaign to make ten thousand new friends by training to be better at hearing and seeing people. Preparation for the show included a teach-in on architectural lighting and an experience called "sonic massage" provided by musician Kenny Wolleson and his homemade instruments. The year after that it was *Don't Let The Sheep Get In Your Eyes,* "an intimate science fiction story knit together with authentic sheep's wool and music." That show was inspired in part by looking at the food element of Yiddish

---

78   Ibid.

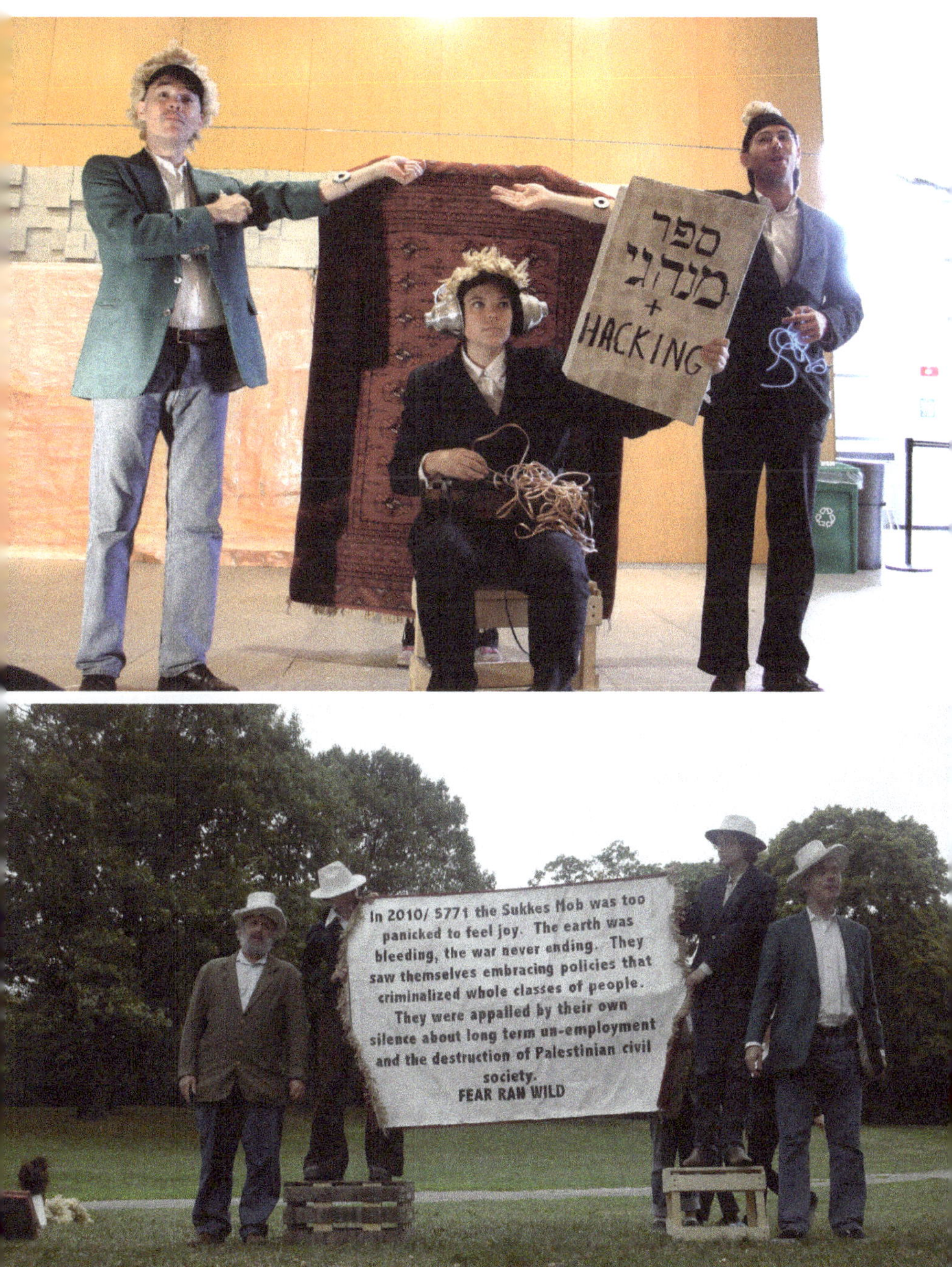

Sukkos Mob, "Don't Let the Sheep Get in Your Eyes" (Photo credit: Bugz Fraugg)

folk culture. How did our ancestors prepare food without using so many fossil fuels? Pickling! Fermentation! The show was also inspired by Michael Chabon's fictional narrative *The Yiddish Policeman's Union* about a Yiddish community in Alaska, and mashed up with Alex Rivera's sci-fi film *Sleep Dealer*, about people being displaced in rural Oaxaca.

In the fall of 2011, the Sukkos Mob performed in the week before Rosh Hashanah, the Jewish New Year, so the troupe used the Sukkot-style performance medium of joyful street theater to tell a story using New Year themes and rituals, woven through with gorgeous traditional music—*Avinu Malkeinu* (a haunting prayer-song beseeching God to grant us justice and salvation), and a remixed version of *Yigdal*, the hymn sung at the end of the New Year's service.

Since Jenny had built a ton of chicken puppets for the Nekhame Epshteyn Chicken Park that summer, chickens were the central characters for a new Sukkos Mob show remixing KlezKanada's *Truth in Gay Clothes: The Musar Musical*. A surrealist narrative unfolds, telling of the Hasidic ritual of *shluggin kapores* in which a chicken is swung overhead while a prayer is recited, asking that the sins of the Jews be driven into the chicken. The chicken is then killed and fed to the poor.

The Sukkos Mob chickens of Brooklyn are not happy! Jenny explains, "Imagine what it's like when your job description is to be killed and eaten for someone else's misconduct!"

To me the metaphor of the *shluggin kapores* was, of course, the chickens saying, "Fuck you, Wall Street. We're not gonna take this fucking austerity that you're shoving down our throats. We're not gonna die for your sins." And so for me it was completely politically interesting to have an insurrection around these chickens.

In the show, we learn that the chickens' anxiety can erupt into compulsive joke-telling, and hear a bunch of great jokes. Suddenly, a giant chicken shows up and we learn that "The Chickens of Brooklyn are liberating themselves using advanced musical theater techniques!" We sing the traditional song *Mene Tekel U-Pharson*, and out of the giant chicken comes a message—a translation of the song: "Your days are numbered. You've been weighed in the balance and found wanting. Your empire will fall. Your goose is cooked!" The chickens go on strike against *shluggin kapores*. The crowd pledges "Monster Chicken of misfires! We promise to interrupt our normal behavior! And to be continuously revolting!"

The narrator of 2011's Sukkos Mob is named "Truth in Gay Clothes," a reference to a story told by Rebbetzin Hadassah Gross, in which Truth is walking around naked and people can't look at him, and everyone runs away from him. He meets Parable on the street, and Parable is gaily decked out in all kinds of finery. Parable explains to Truth that people can't handle things bare, and by dressing up a bit, people will be able to connect with you. Truth let Parable dress him up in some gay clothes and people welcomed him. "Since that time Truth and Parable are to be seen as inseparable companions, esteemed and loved by all." In other words, Parable gives Truth the gift of the dazzle camouflage strategy.

Why make this ritual so clearly queer? Not only because the gay clothes make it easier to witness the revolutionary messages; not only because Jenny is a big queer herself, as are many of the performers and band members; but also because the Mob's visible queerness is a response and resistance to the homophobia of Hasidic Jewish culture—as if to say "here's an alternate reality in which Jews dance all night singing Yiddish on the street but they're actually homos, feminists, and secular anarchists!" Or, as the Sukkos Mob says, FUN IS NOT JUST FOR FUNDAMENTALISTS.

THE RUBBER (CHICKEN) MEETS THE ROAD

The Occupy Wall Street (OWS) movement started on September 17th, 2011. On September 23rd, The Sukkos Mob performed the show *Truth In Gay Clothes or your Goose is Cooked* at St. Ann's Warehouse in the DUMBO neighborhood of Brooklyn as part of the Great Small Works Spaghetti Dinner. The next day—September 24th—the Sukkos Mob took to the streets at the DUMBO Arts Festival. While the chickens were revolting in Brooklyn, Occupy Wall Street marched uptown in Manhattan. Police targeted the OWS marchers—it was their first day of mass arrests. At that point, the OWS protest quickly grew into a huge movement, and the Sukkos Mob showed up to the demonstrations with the chickens. Jenny transcribed lines from the movie *Planet of the Apes*, which she interprets to be about repressed classes revolting, and she replaced the word *ape* with *chicken*—turning those lines into chants for the protests. So the Mob would be at protests with all these chicken puppets, singing *Avinu Malkeinu* and chanting:

> where there's chickens
> there's fire
> where there's fire
> there's smoke

your

days

are numbered

In October 2011, the *New York Times'* Arts and Culture section featured a video of Occupy Wall Street's playful "Occupy Halloween" contingent, building a float and a set of superhero costumes in the Great Small Works studio space. Images of volunteers using papier mâché, staple guns, and sewing machines flash across the screen. Introducing Great Small Works, Jenny explains: "We are a collective of artists and we share our space with all kinds of community groups. Our goal is to keep theater at the heart of social life. And when we make art, we unleash power."

A year later, Hurricane Sandy hit New York on October 28th and 29th, 2012 and the Occupy movement mobilized a response: Occupy Sandy. This led to another example of remixing theatrical spectacle into street mobilization tools. That spring, the Purimshpil was called *Your Homentaschen Are Killing Me! A Purim Ball for the Body, its Resilience, its Fragility, and its Bounce!* and the musical team had created a mash-up of the Yiddish song "Balabuste Zisinke" (an Adrienne Cooper classic, in her memory) and the New Orleans Sissy Bounce song "Excuse" by Big Freedia. As part of Occupy Sandy, a brass band[79] headed out to devastated areas to help draw stranded people's attention to hot food and resources set up by the Occupy volunteers. There, Jenny got everyone to do an irresistible version of the "Excuse" song as a chant:

Excuse

I don't mean to be rude

But I just want to tell you

'bout some free hot food![80]

---

79   Mostly members of the Rude Mechanical Orchestra.
80   As told to me in conversation with Lily Paulina.

Great Small Works' ability to offer a space to the Occupy Wall Street Puppetry Guild in response to immediate need, and the brass band ready to go raise a ruckus to help people find resources during a crisis are examples of how an ongoing radical art practice can unleash power in moments of transformative opportunity.

On a more ongoing basis, Jenny helps bring together art and artists to enliven a campaign as a member of the organization Milk Not Jails. Jenny is an active member of this volunteer-run, grassroots campaign that seeks to build a new urban-rural alliance in New York State, saying, "If rural New York's economic survival depends on my habits, I'd rather drink their milk than go to their prison."[81] Milk Not Jails' two immediate goals are to end upstate New York's dependence on the prison economy (where 90% of New York's prisons are located), and to revitalize and reinvest in the agricultural economy as a model alternative to the prison economy. Milk Not Jails has a dairy brand that distributes goods from farmers who have signed on to their political campaign, to shops and Community Supported Agriculture cooperatives in New York City, where distributors also sign on to the campaign. They raise awareness through a variety of strategies, including presentations to other organizations, their Kickstarter campaign to raise the funds for a refrigerated truck, entering local Upstate Dairy Parades, and events like the Ice Cream Social at Dixon Place in 2011, which advertised a mix of politics and aesthetic delights:

> Milk Not Jails will melt your mind with fresh local ice cream and hot queer political desire. Come to an old-fashioned homosexual ice cream social and learn about what milk and jails have to do with one another. . . . Revel in a garden of glistening glitter cherries, and enjoy the milk drunk antics of the ice cream cone mascot and the Milk Maids of Mars. Look exquisite in our photo booth, wander through the flags, the games, the candy stripes, banners and zines while bathing in an aura of full frozen fat. . . .

---

81   For more information, see: http://milknotjails.wordpress.com

> A creamy cavalcade of stars in the full gender spectrum Dairy Prince/ss pageant. Cool off with live solutions thinking on ice![82]

These moments to "play" with the idea of prison abolition offer another great example of rehearsing resistance. I was especially moved by one of Milk Not Jails' carnival games at the Ice Cream Social, a variation of the traditional darts challenge. A large map of New York State was covered in balloons: red representing prisons, green representing land, and blue representing water. The goal was to pop the red balloons, and each time someone was successful, we got to have the momentary elation of shutting down a prison—a moment to imagine a world with No More Prisons. Then we got to eat ice cream, reminiscent of the Jewish custom of feeding a child honey after their first interaction with the Torah, so that the Torah will be sweet to them.

In the process of rehearsing abolition, we increase our capacity to imagine a world with other options—tasting the sweetness of liberation—and that enables our recommitment to the struggle.

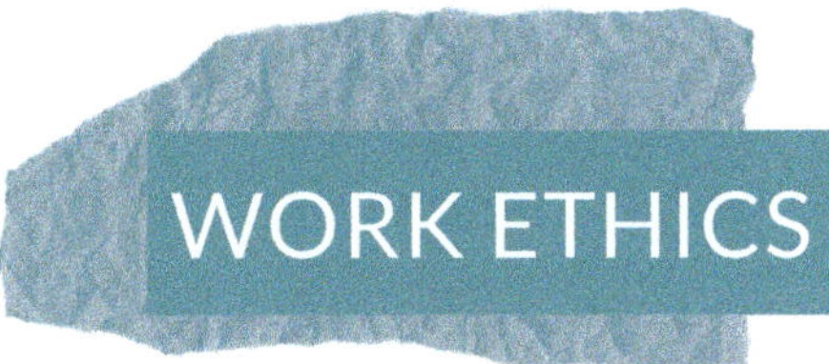

In an interview for the Yiddish Book Center Oral History Project, Pauline Katz asked Jenny Romaine if she has any advice for the next generation. Jenny's answer sums up a number of key themes in her work ethics:

- Trust your instincts.
- Have courage.
- Don't let what other people say define you.

---

82   From the author's personal email, text for July 24, 2011 event flyer.

- Be totally humble.
- Make sure you really understand what you're talking about.
- Do your best to do really rigorous research and partner with people that are more literate and knowledgeable than you.
- Have fun and just know that if it sounds good, it is good.

One thing I want to pull out of this advice is the clear ethic in the instructions: "Make sure you really understand what you're talking about. Do your best to do really rigorous research and partner with people that are more literate and knowledgeable than you." In my work with Jenny, I've come to understand that, perhaps more than any other artist I've personally witnessed, she has a deep understanding of herself not just as a professional artist, but as a cultural *worker*. She says she's "crazy about artistic integrity" and it shows. She comes from the school of heavy lifting as an artist (literally, looking back to her uncle the traveling weight lifter), and she's deeply committed to building work that is a result of careful choices. It may look chaotic. It may be nonlinear, may manifest in experimental, avant-garde, surrealist aesthetics. But her art is always highly structured, deeply researched, and ethically informed. That wasn't clear to me at first. Because it's so much fun to make theater like this, and as I was often coming in at the end of the process, I didn't feel like I was *working*. As I increasingly witnessed and participated in elements of the backstage creation of Jenny's shows, I recognized a trained, practiced professional at work. And Jenny's concerns about capitalism and workers' struggles were also increasingly clear as I got to know her. Because she is a working artist, and we live in a country and an era that doesn't value art as labor, she and all of her colleagues are stuck in a constant hustle to convince curators and producers that their work, their labor and skills, are valuable.

Jenny's passion for layering and mixing is also clear in her joyful descriptions of the groups of colleagues she works with in various jobs or projects. She is consistently found mixing together wildly diverse, intergenerational groups of people, and directing a collaborative cultural mash-up with all of their input. In part, this reflects learning from her experiences in Bread and Puppet and YIVO, but it's also connected to her advice: "Do your best to do really rigorous research and partner with people that are more literate and knowledgeable than you." Part of how we can make powerful, ethical theater is by connecting with other people who can fill in their piece of the content. Like when singer Galit Dardashdi taught Jewish Iranian Sukkot songs and Persian songs about water to The Sukkos Mob, or when Domestic Workers United collaborated on a Purimshpil script about the domestic workers of Shushan. Itzik Gottesman, Shane Baker, Jeffrey Shandler, Loren Sklamberg, and—until her death in 2011—Adrienne Cooper, are all crucial content providers from Yiddishland. Judith Berkson, Avi Fox-Rosen, and Michelle Miller are all regular Jewish content providers as well.

Jenny learned from YIVO that there's no limit to what we can understand as a Jewish text, or source. We can look at the rituals, the people, all of the materials, and we can ask questions and come up with answers together, through exploring these materials. And each new project is an opportunity to build new collaborative relationships and collective learning in the ethnographic-collection process.

In December 2011, I went to KlezKamp as a work-study assistant for Jenny's Youth Theater Workshop. A couple of weeks out, we started discussing ideas for the show and how to stage it. With three or four days to make a show with teenagers and adolescents, I learned, you need to do a lot of prep work. Jenny usually takes a van full of props and creative materials to the gathering space but that year she was going to ride the charter bus, so we needed to figure out how to create visual transformation with just a few suitcases of supplies. Projections! She packed a couple of projectors and some colored gels, blank transparencies to print and draw on, and her computer could hook up to the projector for a slide show. If necessary, she could go into town and clear out the sale-rack of Christmas decorations on December 26th. We read the text of a children's story about a revolutionary dog that she had chosen to focus the show on, and generated a list of visual elements from the reading: snow, the color red ("that's complicated because some of the attendees are survivors of Communism in Russia"), police, cardboard signs, the telepathy of dogs. This is a Yiddish Folk Arts camp, she explained, so we would have to be selective about any content elements not related to Yiddish culture.

In our conversations, Jenny mentioned artistic influences including William Kentridge, Vsevolod Meyerhold, and the Artef Theater. In the week before the gathering, I frantically did homework to try to acquaint myself with these references.

That week at KlezKamp was the first time I had witnessed Jenny's process of creating a show from start to finish. Her professionalism, her experienced insights, and her wild creativity had never been more clear to me. And at the same time, I saw new elements of how she teaches and encourages leadership from all participants, regardless of age.

No wonder, then, that she now works closely with a group of adults who grew up with KlezKamp. And after a decade of building spectacles with her, I realized that I had also grown up as an artist in the school of Jenny Romaine. Over ten years since I first stepped onto a stage under Jenny's direction, I can't imagine how different my life, my art, my activism would be without these experiences, without Jenny's modeling of exactly how art unleashes power.

DREAMING IN YIDDISH

In 2013, I was honored to introduce Jenny as the first recipient of the Adrienne Cooper Dreaming in Yiddish Award. I spoke of Jeffrey Shandler's reference of Yiddishland as a place that doesn't appear on maps, but comes into existence whenever people speak Yiddish. Shandler complicates this description, asking:

> Does Yiddishland flicker on and off during a conversation, vanishing during pauses and interruptions? … Does talking to oneself in Yiddish constitute Yiddishland, or is some sort of community, even a community of two, required? And what about thinking or dreaming in Yiddish?[83]

Especially for those of us who don't have conversational skills, dreaming in Yiddish is one of the ways we can enter Yiddishland. In our waking lives, we can also enter through the collective dreamscapes that emerge from the New Yiddish Theater of Jenny Romaine. This world of moving images, mashed-up musical montages, swimming symbols, and folkloric fantasia offers us a portal into Yiddishland, an entryway that jumps from Long Island's Jewish day schools to a busy Times Square intersection, to a borscht belt hotel, and then springs up again down under the Manhattan Bridge. Where else but in a Yiddish dreamscape could we meet a chicken version of YIVO *aspirant* Nekhame Epshteyn, and offer her a joke for her ethnographic collection? How else could we find our-

---

83   Shandler, *Adventures in Yiddishland*, 33-34.

selves at a body of water simultaneously in the mountains outside of Montreal and in Stanashest, Rumania, playing klezmer music with 400 people, walking backwards together in procession?

Speaking with some of my peers who have also been learning with Jenny over the past decade, we've identified a profound theme in our experiences: Jenny offers us the illuminating clarity that who we are has a legacy—that our experimental creative visions, our queerness, our yearning and our organizing for justice on a collective level have a rich history in Yiddishland. We are making new culture, and we also come from somewhere. We have a past *and a future*. Jenny shows us that what we have in Yiddishland is our fragments of culture, and the role of the artist is to bring our whole selves to the task of rearranging those fragments. In doing so, we make a new wholeness.

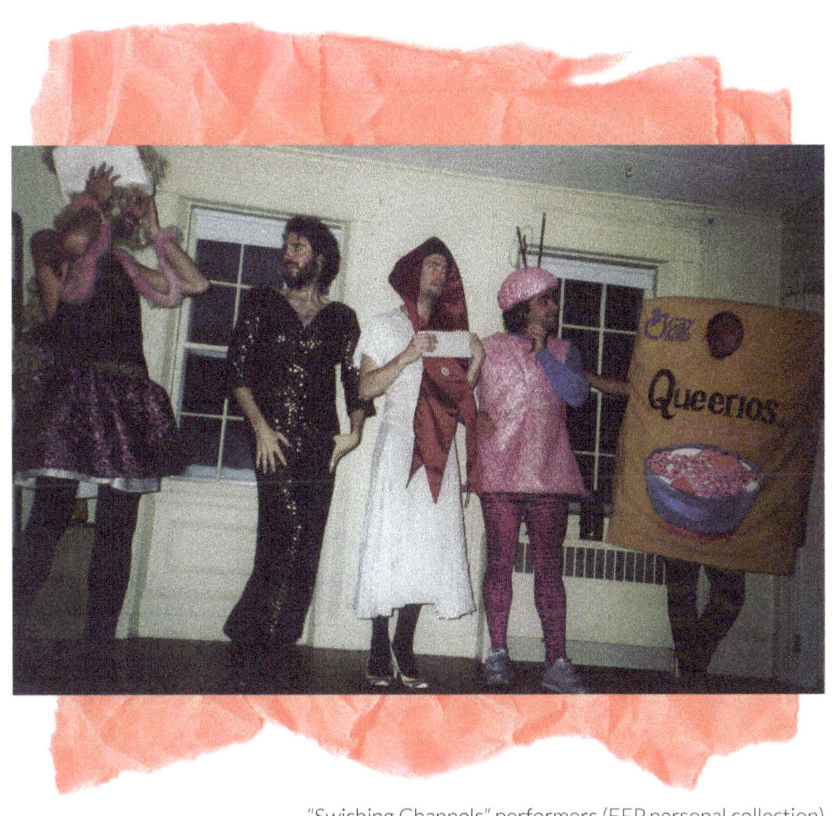

"Swishing Channels" performers (EFP personal collection)

INTRODUCING THE EGGPLANT FAERIE PLAYERS

Spotlight up on a villainous executive of the drug company Hale-Bopp Pharmaceuticals, talking with his two henchmen:

> Executive: For fifteen years, our sales have been growing. Our profits have been growing *[evil laugh]*. BUT THEY'RE NOT GROWING FAST ENOUGH!"

One of the henchmen explains that since losing the monopoly on protease inhibitors, AIDS just isn't profitable anymore. They need new drugs. They need new diseases—quick! A new form of asthma! A hemorrhoid epidemic! They need to come up with new treatments for ailments affecting people with health insurance—no more unprofitable drugs for diseases of the impoverished, starving, and uninsured. On top of this, the businessman bellows, ever since that alien spaceship—The Mothership—has arrived, it has bestowed good health on everyone!

> Executive: For fifteen years, I personally supervised the manufacturing and marketing of some of the most expensive drugs in the history of human kind. Drugs that were each hailed at one point or another as the new cure for AIDS [*evil laugh*]. And all of the sudden this "M" [Queen of the Mothership] thinks she can come along and take this from me. Who does she think she is? Does she know what I had to do to get to where I am? Does she know what it took to gain the respect, power, and clout which are mine today?

The Executive and henchmen take off their villain outfits and uncover masculine jeans and T-shirts. They march in unison, joined by other cast members. Together, each wearing a different color shirt, they form a marching rainbow. They sing to the beat of their stomping march:

> Executive:
> Does she even know what it was like to grow up and be all alone
> When all the other children always called me names?

They called me a faggot, said I throw like a girl
And they never ever let me be a part of their games

And then when I grew up and realized I'm gay
I went to the gym until my body was strong
And I could pretend that if I behaved like them
Then maybe maybe, maybe they would let me belong

To the powerful clout
Of the rich and the snobs
The wealthy privileged ones
The rulers of the world

I put on a suit
I danced to their flute
And I never, never let them see me throw like a girl

Chorus:
So hide the transexuals
We'll hide the bisexuals
We'll hide the fats, we'll hide the femmes, and those whose dick
is too small
We'll hide the outrageous ones
We'll hide the contagious ones
It's the price of equality
Cause our goal
Is liberty for all

So just be nice
Put your feelings on ice
And spare us the gory details
Of what you do in bed
We'll never ask
And I'll never tell

We'll smoke cigars and drive big cars
And everything will be swell

There's a place at the table
The American fable
They'll open the gates
We'll act like it's great
Imagine what I could get

You can serve in the army
You could make lots of money
You could marry your spouse and buy a big house
With a lawn and a credit card debt

And all I have to do is just
Hide the transexuals
The flaming bisexuals
We'll hide the fats, we'll hide the femmes, and those whose dick
is too small
We'll hide the outrageous ones
We'll hide the contagious ones
If the price looks small
It's cause our goal
Is liberty for all[84]

This scene is from the Eggplant Faerie Players' 1997 show *Dial M for Mothership*, set in the future, at the end of the millennium when the Hale-Bopp comet has arrived with a spaceship (the Mothership) trailing behind it. The spaceship's engine is called the Ryan White[85] Innocent

---

84   Transcribed by author from a highlights reel DVD.

85   Ryan White was an Indiana teenager and hemophiliac who was diagnosed with HIV in 1984, contracted through a blood transfusion. He died in 1990 at age eighteen. White's HIV status brought awareness to a wide public that HIV was not only a gay disease. Congress passed the Ryan White Care Act shortly after his death, the largest source of funding for US HIV/AIDS service organizations.

Victims Lounge. There, the souls of everyone who has died of AIDS party in an endless rave which generates the energy to fuel the Mothership. Besides bringing good health for all, the Mothership also brings peace on earth so there's no longer need for religion, and it makes everyone gay by sprinkling fairy dust from the sky.

The scene is a great example of the group's style. Portraying drug companies as evil profiteers leads into a critique of gay conformity in the chase of power. As Eggplant Faerie member Dashboard explains:

> The issues we address in our shows are often the same: the commercializing of our culture, the pressure to conform (especially in the gay community), the connection between militarism and religious fanaticism. But we try to not take ourselves too seriously. As faeries, we are the first to make fun of pretentiousness—especially our own. Faeries like to play and goof around a lot. When on stage, we ritualize our goofiness, recreating it over and over in our performances.
>
> [Eggplant Faerie Player] TomFoolery calls this the role of the sacred clown. The sacred clown's purpose is to bring authority down to earth, to strip the emperor's clothes. Our experience of otherness—not only as gay people in a hetero world, but as freaks in the gay "community"—allows us to see and express what other people might not notice or maybe choose to ignore.[86]

Who are the Eggplant Faerie Players? How did they come to make this goofy, weird, political queer theater? Their stories interweave with the evolution of the Radical Faerie community, and the development of the AIDS epidemic.

---

86 Nettles [aka Dashboard] "Eggplant Faerie Players Profile," *Radical Faerie Digest*, Summer 2003 (#114, Radically Fine Designers), 27.

ENTER SPREE

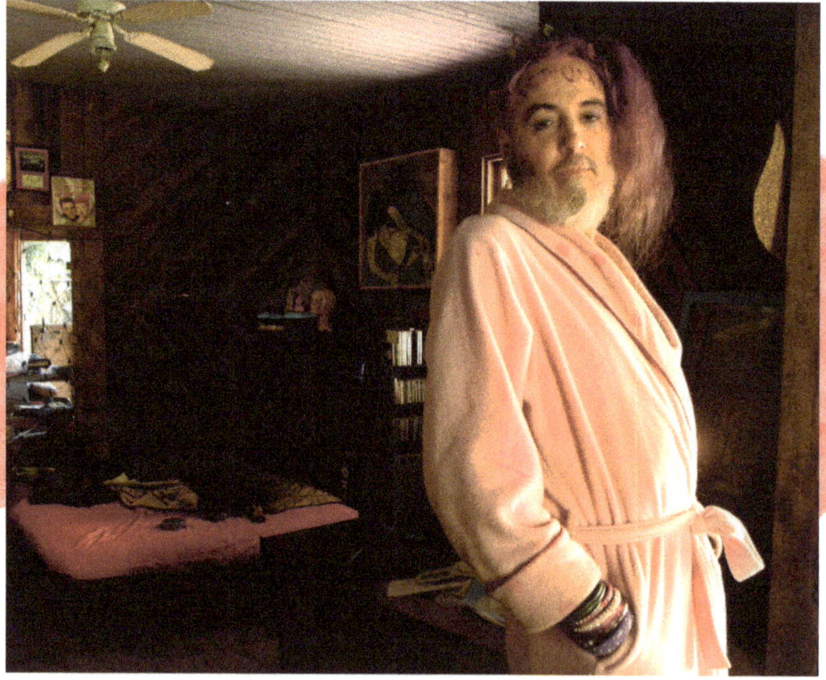

SPREE, 2011 (Photo credit: Rosin Bean James)

Today, SPREE[87] is a bearded queen in her late 50s, always decked out with purple hair and beard, flowing pink or purple dresses, arms laden elbow to wrist with sparkly bangle bracelets, jewel-ringed fingers, and painted purple nails. In addition to her glimmering glamour as a blur of

---

87   SPREE prefers to spell her name with all capital letters, and does not have a pronoun preference, but will use "she" if forced to choose.

pink and purple, she is always trailed by a train of devoted dog friends—I think of her as "Our Lady of the Canines."

SPREE grew up in Houston, Texas until the age of ten and then moved to Southern Georgia, "from a bad situation to a worse situation"[88] for a young queer person. SPREE moved to Los Angeles at seventeen, in 1975, to attend the American Academy of Dramatic Arts. She stayed in LA for the next ten years, working phone switchboard jobs to support her acting career. "Some people wait tables, some people bartend, I did phone jobs" says SPREE. She also attended support groups at the Gay and Lesbian Community Services Center,[89] however, SPREE explains, "coming out and trying to be a movie star did not go hand in hand at that time, because it was the pre–Rock Hudson[90] era."

SPREE found the newly emerging Radical Faerie movement in the summer of 1983 when she attended a gathering outside San Diego. She remembers, "Once I met the Faeries, it became pretty clear to me that it was a lot more important to be who I am as a person than to try to play this Hollywood game of hiding myself so that I could be a movie star." SPREE got increasingly more involved with the Faeries and in 1985 she decided to leave LA, initiating a period of travel that led her to the Spring Gathering at a Radical Faerie intentional community in Tennessee. She eventually settled down in New York with friends, fellow Faerie performers Agnes de Garron[91] and Gabriel Quirk, and found work on the switchboard at NBC at 30 Rockefeller Center.

88   SPREE, interviewed by Sarah Schulman for ACT UP's Oral History Project, 2006.
89   Spree says, "My first boyfriend worked at the gay center. And we actually got up there, on the roof, and stuck in another sign that said, 'Lesbian,' so it would say 'Gay and Lesbian Community Services Center.'" [From her ACT UP oral history interview.]
90   Rock Hudson was a movie star from the 1950s to the 1980s who was closeted until acknowledging he had AIDS in the summer of 1985, having been diagnosed a year earlier (he died that fall). Rock Hudson coming out, as a movie star known and loved by Hollywood and the US public, was a watershed event in the visibility and public perception of HIV/AIDS.
91   Agnes de Garron is a dancer, choreographer, performer and a longtime Radical Faerie. He is a founding member of the Sisters of Perpetual Indulgence, a group of psychedelic nuns that formed in San Francisco following the first Radical Faerie gathering in 1979. As a Sister, she has been known as Sister BananaNutBread, Sister Hysterectoria, and Sister Solicitation. For more on Agnes' story, see Michael Lecker, "Transcription of 'History of

RESPONDING TO AIDS

In March of 1983, the year SPREE got involved with the Radical Faeries, writer and activist Larry Kramer wrote an article titled "1,112 and Counting," sounding an alarm about the rapidly climbing number of AIDS cases.[92]

Reading through back issues of *Radical Faerie Digest (RFD)*[93], I found that the first feature on AIDS came in the Winter 1985 issue (#45, "Re-Forming Diet")[94]—with a wide variety of information: AIDS news, resources, and info numbers; a focus on holistic and alternative treatments to AIDS; Crazy Owl's "Holistic Alternatives to the Epidemic of Fear"; Harold R. Cole's "Defusing AIDS Panic"; a report of a channeled reading about AIDS; a report on one man who had recovered from AIDS; and a proposal for bathhouses to serve as safe-sex information sites. The issue has a secondary focus on exploring what it means to be in Faerie community.

A year later, in the Winter 1986 issue (#49, "Reimbursed for Dreaming"), the editors' letter reflected on reader controversy and feedback

---

the Faeries.'" http://itwascuriosity.wordpress.com/2012/01/23/transcription-of-history-of-the-faeries. See also: http://www.stageclick.com/person/17200.aspx.
92   Larry Kramer, "1,112 and Counting," *New York Native* 14 (1983).
93   *RFD* is a reader-written journal for gay people which focuses on country living and encourages alternative lifestyles. Founded in 1974, *RFD* continues to put out quarterly (seasonal) issues named in some combination of words with the acronym of RFD. *RFD* pre-dates the creation of Radical Faerie community but has come to be closely associated. More information at www.rfdmag.org.
94   Compiled by Sister Missionary Position, aka Sr. Mish, aka Sr. Soami, one of the founders of the Sisters of Perpetual Indulgence.

over whether the alternative health care angle on AIDS in *RFD* was misleading and dangerous. An article by Billy Russo identified the current moment as a third stage of the epidemic, when AIDS had begun to reach beyond large cities and gay cultural centers, and second-tier gay cities, to rural communities.

By the end of 1987, there were 50,378 cases of AIDS reported in the US and 40,849 deaths.[95]

The AIDS Coalition to Unleash Power (ACT UP) was founded in March 1987, kicking off with a March on Wall Street. In October of that year, the second National March on Washington for Lesbian and Gay Rights was attended by an estimated half-million people, led by People with AIDS.[96] It was also the first public display of the AIDS Quilt. A few days later, SPREE was one of almost 600 people arrested in the first national lesbian and gay civil disobedience action at the Supreme Court, in protest of the homophobic Bowers v. Hardwick ruling, which affirmed a Georgia sodomy law as constitutional—criminalizing gay sex, including sex in private and between consenting adults.[97] From the *New York Times* report on the demonstration:

> At one point, a group of demonstrators including some AIDS victims [sic] sat down on the steps of the building and began to chant, "We have AIDS, and we have rights." At another, as a group crossed the barricades to be arrested, some police officers at the top of the steps placed white gloves on their hands, ostensibly as a protection against AIDS, prompting the crowd to shout, "Shame, shame!" and "Your gloves don't match your shoes!"[98]

95   "Thirty Years of HIV/AIDS: Snapshots of an Epidemic." *Amfar,The Foundation for AIDS Research.* http://www.amfar.org/thirty-years-of-hiv/aids-snapshots-of-an-epidemic/
96   The largest mass arrest at the Supreme Court since May Day in 1971, when 7,000 antiwar protesters were detained, from Lena Williams, "600 in Gay Demonstration Arrested at Supreme Court," *New York Times*, October 14, 1987. For more information, see: http://www.glbtq.com/social-sciences/marches_washington.html.
97   This ruling was not overturned until 2003's *Lawrence v. Texas* case.
98   Williams, "600 in Gay Demonstration Arrested."

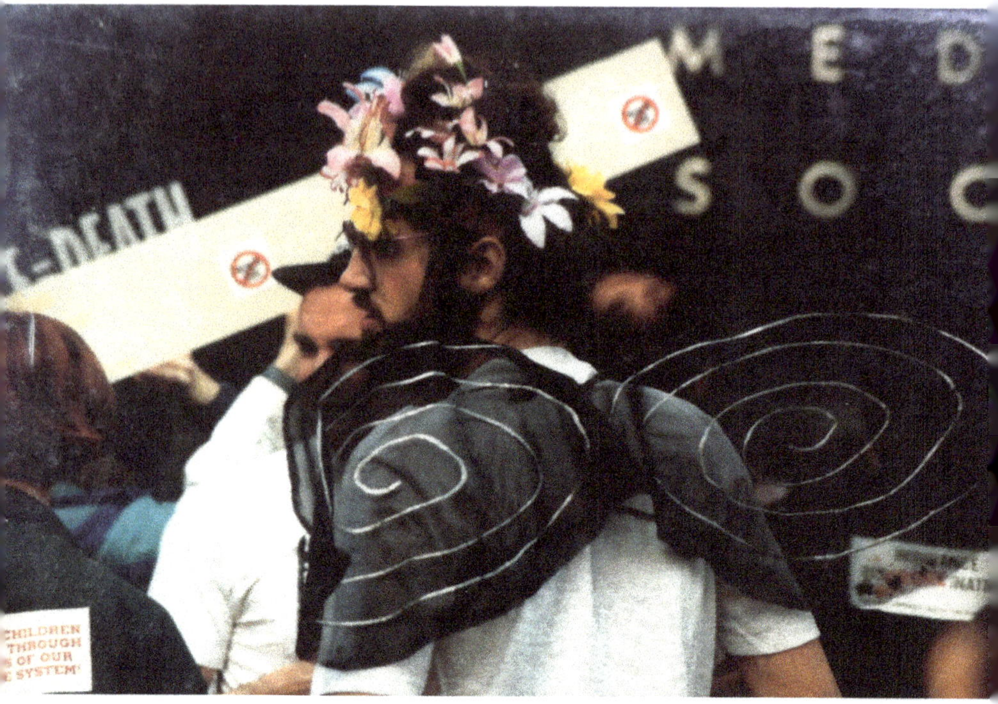

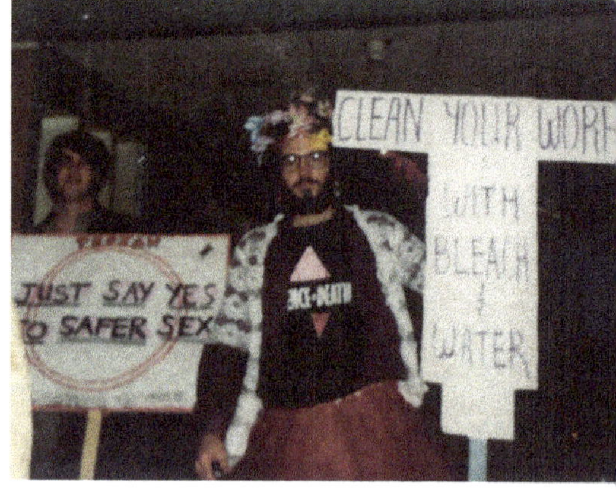

SPREE in ACT UP demonstration (EFP personal collection)

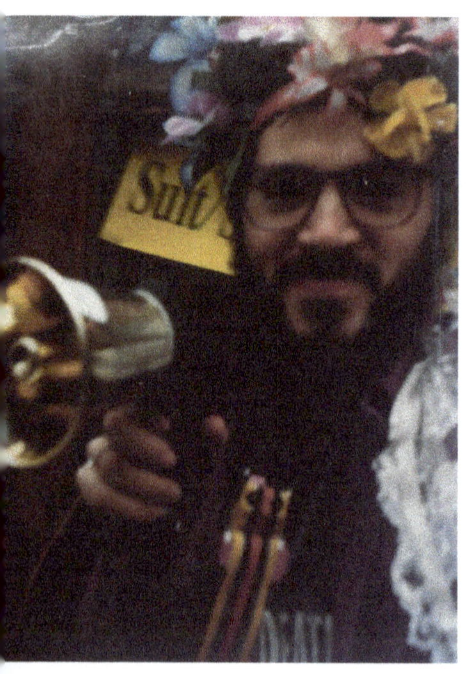

[Left] SPREE at ACT UP Protest (EFP personal collection)

[Above] SPREE at ACT UP Ann Arbor demonstration (EFP personal collection)

SPREE had attended the action with Faerie friends, not planning to get arrested, but swept up in the excitement she joined the resisting group and was put on a police bus with Ortez Alderson, Gregg Bordowitz, and many other ACT UP members. SPREE was one of two people who refused to enter a formal "not guilty" plea, instead telling the judge, "We plead for a reversal of the Supreme Court's decision of Bowers versus Hardwick." SPREE went to trial, in drag as always, but none of the cops showed up because they were providing security for Russian President Mikhail Gorbachev's Washington, DC visit. The judge dropped the charges, and a crowd of activists was there to celebrate with her. That's how she got involved with ACT UP.

As was widely true for ACT UP members, the political network also became an intimate community. SPREE had a blowout 30th birthday party shortly after her arrest in DC, and that night sparked a romance with Gregg Bordowitz. She also developed a very close friendship with Ortez Alderson, and she joined the Metropolitan Health Association (MHA) affinity group which both Ortez and Gregg were involved in. SPREE says of Ortez, "[He was] probably the most politically—you know when you say affinity group—the most politically aligned with anybody I ever was in my life." Because of her phone switchboard experience and her activism, SPREE became one of the first staff members of the National AIDS Hotline and was able to hire Ortez and other ACT UP members to her shift. They teamed up on many ACT UP actions including crashing a Republican Ladies' Tea Party during the 1988 George H.W. Bush presidential campaign.

Working the overnight shift at the Hotline, SPREE was on the receiving end of many calls from people who had worked themselves into a frenzy about unlikely ways they might have been exposed to the virus. These calls included queries such as: "If a person from the country visits the big city and gets it, then goes back to the country and gives it to a cow, can I get it from eating a hamburger?" Says SPREE, "This was in the early days when people literally didn't know anything about AIDS. The

Hotline was advertised on TV—if you have a question about AIDS, call this 800 number—and I was answering those calls."

SPREE performed dramatic renditions of the most outrageous hotline calls, bringing humor to the crisis of silence and misinformation about AIDS transmission and treatment options. At ACT UP's anniversary parties, she performed in character as Barbara Broadcast, a tripped-out take on Lily Tomlin's phone-operator character Ernestine. Always in Faerie drag, SPREE brought her full self to her life as an AIDS activist, including her trial with the Surrender, Dorothy Affinity Group of ACT UP NY, which took their name from a message sky-written by the wicked witch in *The Wizard of Oz*.

Surrender, Dorothy was focused on NYC Health Commissioner Stephen Joseph, whose irresponsible behavior included suddenly halving the number of estimated AIDS cases in NYC—which would inevitably lead to dramatically reduced funding for AIDS services. ACT UP NY got a copy of Joseph's itinerary and shut him down at every appointment. In her interview with the ACT UP Oral History Project, SPREE reports on an action where the affinity group interrupted a meeting between Joseph and a number of city health officials. In a "very lovely black and white polka-dot dress and pink sunglasses,"[99] SPREE took Joseph's seat when he got up, screaming protest chants and banging her fists so hard she broke one of her rings.

Eventually that affinity group went to trial—a three-week trial—and SPREE had a different dramatic outfit for every day. She and her co-workers and co-defendents Ortez Alderson and Bill Monahan would work all night at the AIDS Hotline and then get off in the morning, get on the train, and go downtown to the courtroom at 100 Centre Street. In anticipation of the sentencing, and her opportunity to give a sentencing statement, SPREE decided to reenact the glamour of a scene from the end of *Dynasty*'s first season, where Alexis Carrington (Joan Collins)

---

99   ACT UP Oral History interview.

dramatically enters a courtroom in a big hat. "So I came in with my big hat," says SPREE, "a lovely hat to match my outfit."

> The bailiff comes over and he says, "Excuse me, but I'm going to have to ask you to take off that hat." And I just looked at him, and I said, "Well answer me this: if I was a woman would you ask me to take off my hat?" and he said "Actually, yes I would" and I said "Well then, in that case I *shall* take it off." But if he had said that a woman *could* wear it, I was gonna *pitch a bitch* and *not* willingly remove my hat!"

The Surrender, Dorothy members all made impassioned statements, explains SPREE:

> Originally when the judge sentenced us she said "you broke the law, and because of that you should be punished, so I'm sentencing you to ten days with the Department of Sanitation." And we were like, "Uh, excuse me, some people have HIV and some people have AIDS and you can not be sentencing those kind of people to schlepping with the Department of Sanitation." I thought "there's no way we're ever gonna get through to this woman," but because of the sentencing statements she literally changed her mind. She said "OK, you have convinced me."

The group was sentenced to ten days with AIDS service organization God's Love We Deliver.

ENTER MAXZINE

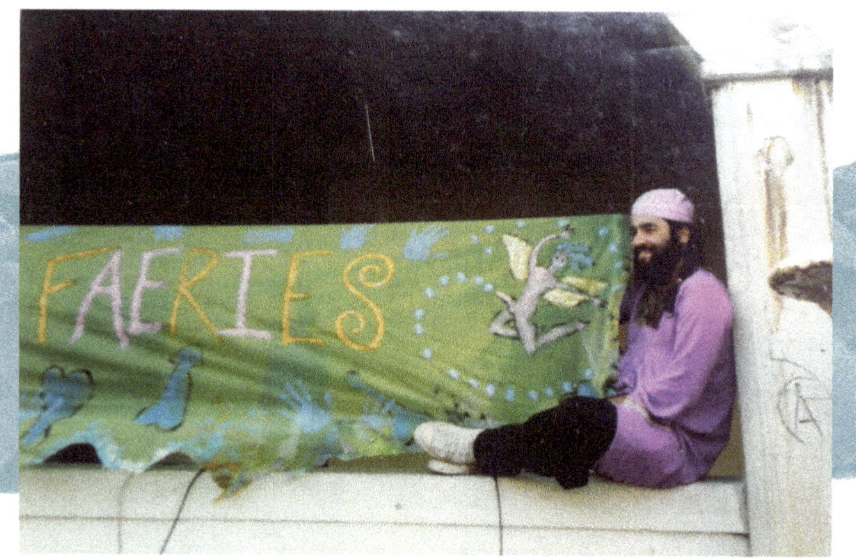

MaxZine with Radical Faeries banner (EFP personal collection)

SPREE and MaxZine Weinstein met at a Radical Faerie gathering at Blue Heron Farm in upstate New York on Labor Day weekend 1988. MaxZine lived in Ann Arbor, Michigan and SPREE in New York City. They began a long-distance romance—they can be seen holding hands in video from ACT UP's action to shut down the FDA a month later.[100]

MaxZine grew up in a Jewish family in Long Island, and his family moved to Iowa when he was fifteen. Looking for activist community, in 1983 he

---

100 *How to Survive a Plague*, directed by David France, 2012.

went to the University of Michigan in Ann Arbor—where Students for a Democratic Society (SDS) was founded in 1960. Once there, he learned that the university was cutting many of the progressive programs he was interested in and had taken on a number of military contracts. He joined up with the Progressive Student Network to challenge the university's connections with the military industry, and he got involved with the Pinkerton Theater Group, where he learned about political street theater.

MaxZine also joined the Latin American Student Solidarity Committee (LASSC), and through that group he participated in an international peace march from Panama to Mexico in 1985 and '86. In Costa Rica, the marchers were attacked by a CIA-funded, anti-Communist group. That attack, and the whole tour, led MaxZine to reevaluate his life when he got back to Ann Arbor, and he dropped out of college to commit to social justice work. In the spring of 1987, he went to Guatemala to work with Peace Brigades International as an escort for the families of the disappeared.

Also, around this time, MaxZine started living as an openly gay man, and was dismayed by the challenge of finding radical groups that weren't homophobic, or queers that cared about politics. Finding the Radical Faeries, and through them getting involved with ACT UP, was a process of finding a place where he could be his whole self. MaxZine was inspired by SPREE's way of consistently bringing theater to her politics. Through SPREE, MaxZine witnessed the power of dazzle camouflage to amplify the reach of political messages.

I would never want to take anything away from how effective some of the ACT UP stuff was, but I find "2! 4! 6! 8! We're gonna say the same chant today!" kind of boring. And I don't like creating totally "us versus them" scenarios, even though clearly people who are oppressed some way should be challenging what's now called the 1% or whatever. But I think people need to keep their motivation up to stay involved, and creativity is one way to do that. If you're like: "We're angry! We're righteous! We're really gonna show you!" a lot of people can block it off. That's my experience anyway, it's like "Okay, yeah, they're protesting." I can't tell you how many times in my life I've heard people say "What are you out here protesting?" And already then you're boxed in, you're a caricature of a protester. I loved seeing what SPREE was doing—not only SPREE but especially SPREE—bringing so much humor to ACT UP New York. SPREE's roommates weren't so into ACT UP, but they'd occasionally dress up and go, and when the three of them went, you could see how the public totally responds differently.

EMMA GOLDMAN GYPSY PLAYERS

In the spring of 1989 the AIDS Hotline closed its NYC office and SPREE went to Michigan to surprise MaxZine on his birthday. They bought a van together and decided to travel the country, performing at gatherings.

In 1989, while temporarily living in San Francisco, SPREE tested positive for HIV. With no way to predict what the coming years would bring, the couple returned to touring. While "tripping in a pool of water" at a Rainbow Gathering, they made a decision to take their performances into broader communities. They soon came up with a vision for a show and sent an advertising flyer to all the groups listed in the Gay Yellow Pages.

SPREE: We just started sending this flyer out to all these groups all around the country, saying "You should have us come perform for you, we're fabulous and you need us and your group would love us." And lo and behold, all these people started answering.

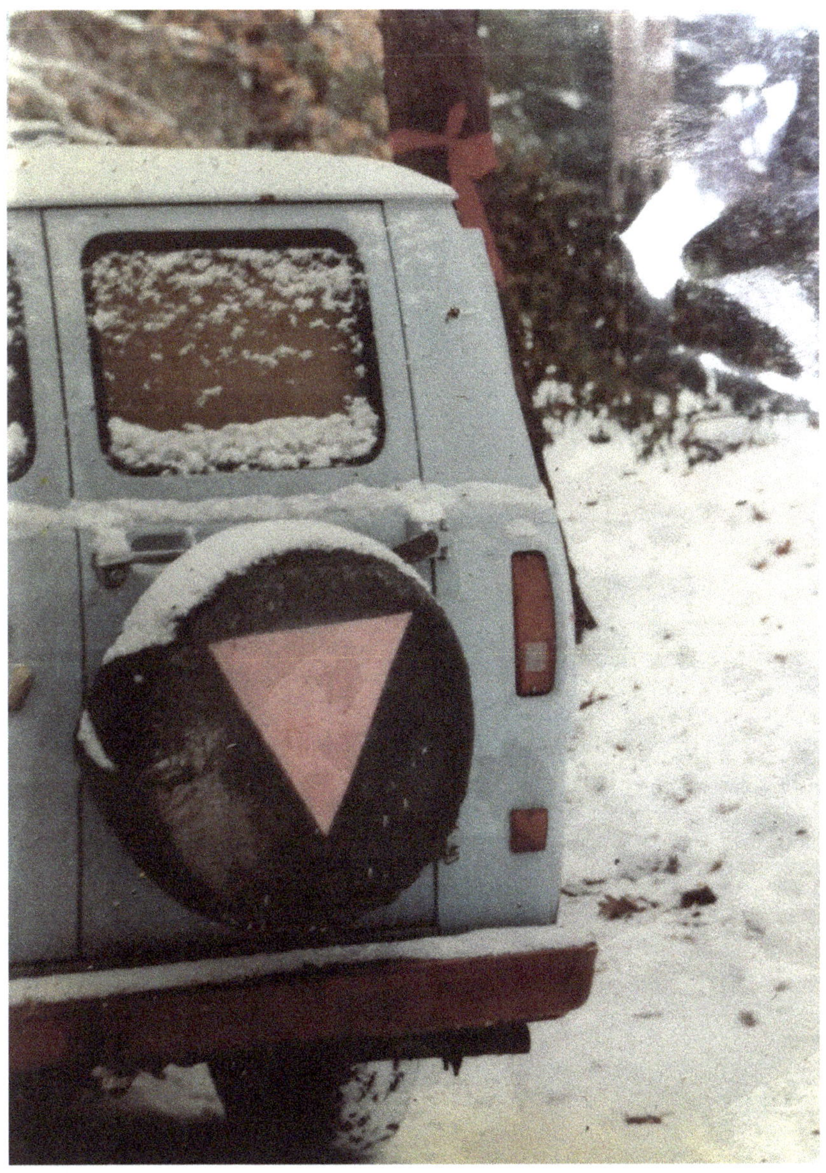

Eggplant Faerie Players' tour van (EFP personal collection)

> They were like "Yes! Please! We want you to come perform for us!" . . . Back then there weren't really traveling gay theater troupes, and people were just starved.[101]

They toured around the country for a year with a show called *Fairy Tails, Faerie Tales*, which was a collection of vaudeville-esque skits including Barbara Broadcast's stories. They took gigs as they came—mostly performing for community and college groups—saying yes to anyone that invited them, zigzagging across the country to places that had never seen gay theater. They occasionally got paid a little by the organizations, passed the hat for gas money, and slept on a lot of couches. Fellow faeries Ian Parabacchus Emma Nanda (aka P.B.) and B.J. Atanasco joined the tour, and Michael Smith of Toronto joined up with his show *Person Livid with AIDS*.

They took the name "Emma Goldman Gypsy Players," which was inspired by MaxZine reading Emma Goldman's 1914 anarchist writing about "theater as political dynamite"[102] and a 1990 production of the musical *Gypsy* at a Tennessee faerie gathering, starring SPREE as the character Mama Rose and SPREE's former roommate, Agnes, as the title character Gypsy Rose Lee. But the reference to Emma Goldman wasn't always clear to audiences—lots of people had never heard of her, and this created some funny moments of confusion.

> MaxZine: We had a phone card, but no one could call us because there weren't cell phones. My mom, who's really sweet, was willing to take messages for us and be our contact. I swear we'd go do shows and way more than once people would be like "who's

---

101 They do remember being inspired by gay singing duo Romanovsky and Phillips, who helped to create a gay touring circuit. They also reference pro-gay and AIDS activist a cappella group The Flirtations, and the Bloolips and Hot Peaches queer/drag performance troupes as early inspirations.

102 "It is the dynamite which undermines superstition, shakes the social pillars, and prepares men and women for the reconstruction." Emma Goldman, *The Social Significance of the Modern Drama* (Boston: R.G. Badger, 1914), 8.

Emma Goldman, is that the lady I talked to on the phone?" We'd say no, that's Judy.

I found a great write-up about this first tour in the Spring 1991 *Radical Faerie Digest*. Agnes de Garron's "Agnes Knows" gossip column gives the scoop:

> Winding up their grand tour of twenty-five states, they ended up doing their special brand of comedy and satire (whole grain with lots of roughage) at the Massachusetts Institute of Technology this past December. [The troupe] received glittering reviews from Boston's Gay Press. Talking about their "crazy carnival atmosphere," their ability to "disarm" their audiences while "celebrating the pleasures of cross-dressing." The manic SPREE Vance, along with the promising Mark Weinstein [MaxZine] have joined the poignant B.J. Atanasco to become a trio more well endowed than the N.E.A.[103]

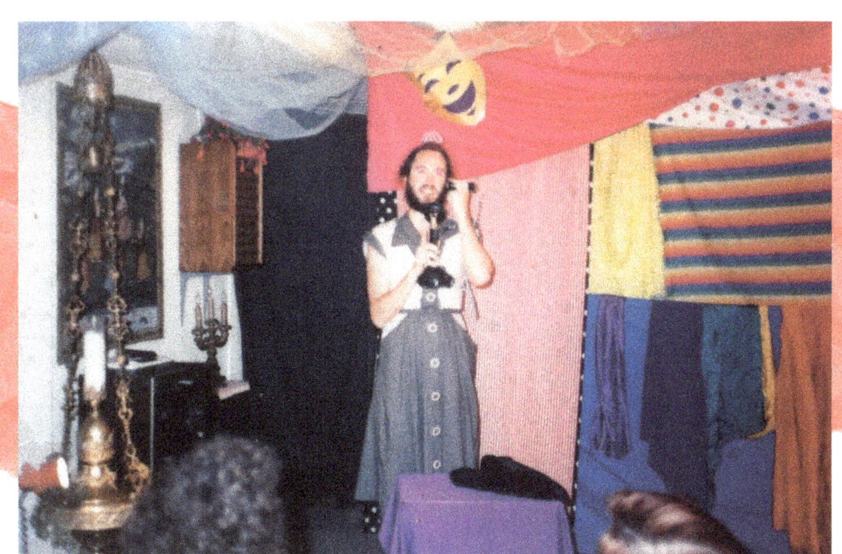

Spree in an early tour performance as Barbara Broadcast (EFP personal collection)

---

103 N.E.A is National Endowment for the Humanities. Agnes de Garron, "Agnes Knows," *Radical Faerie Digest* 65 (Spring 1991).

SPREE and MaxZine took the show on tour to Europe with a first stop at the International Lesbian and Gay Association conference in Copenhagen. While in Copenhagen, they learned that their dear friend Ortez had died.

> SPREE: At the end of the first night, MaxZine got up and said "I've received today the first telegram I've ever gotten in my life and I would like to read it." And he read it, telling us that this very close friend of mine from ACT UP and the AIDS Hotline—and we were in affinity groups together and we were really tight—had died. And I mean there was not a dry eye in the house by the time he finished reading the telegram.

Back in the US, MaxZine and SPREE went to Chicago and joined Ortez's partner Arthur Gursch in spreading Ortez's ashes, keeping some in a little box that traveled around in the Eggplant Faerie Player van on their tours.

Soon after returning from that tour, MaxZine, SPREE, and BJ wrote a new two-act play exploring the tensions between caring for dying friends and on-the-street activism. Barbara Broadcast was back, and the show centered on two drag queens playing canasta with a character named Abby Fein, Jewish mother of their friend who has recently died of AIDS.[104] In the show, the queens try to convince the mother to respect her son's wishes. Abby Fein is not hearing it, and Barbara Broadcast gets more and more annoyed. When Abby goes to the bathroom, the queens spike her drink with Pink Triangle LSD. That's the end of the first act.

Queens Are Wild was a response to the Eggplant Faeries' frustration, witnessing that sometimes people could mobilize all kinds of public demands and get attention for the cause, but didn't know how to be present as caregivers. They understood that some people had some skills

---

104 I wonder if this name is intended to sound like "I'll be fine?"

and some people had others, but they wanted a more holistic movement—one without a gulf between activists and caregivers—that would take the needs of really sick people into account and respect their wishes in activism and in their process of dying.

They also wanted to challenge the ways that AIDS activism was already starting to be packaged for mainstream consumption in the early 1990s.

> MaxZine: It was a period when you could really start seeing the intense AIDS commercialism that was about to come and the red ribbon was already getting branded. And the [AIDS] Quilt, which I love in so many ways—it's so touching—but . . . you know they had just built this air-conditioned warehouse in San Francisco for the Quilt, that cost so much money. But there were homeless gay people dying in the streets who weren't getting the same resources. And it's nothing against the Quilt, and I support arts and arts funding, but it was like "why will our community put so many resources into certain things but not the same resources into the people who are the most vulnerable?"

The show opened in Boston to a controversy. A woman of Romani ethnicity wrote a scathing article in *Gay Community News*, angry about the group's use of the word "Gypsy" in their name. MaxZine remembers, "We were like oh my god we just really like Ethel Merman and Rosalind Russell and *Gypsy*! [*Singing*:] "Clear the decks, light the lights . . . !" As it turns out, SPREE is "half-Gypsy," though that had nothing to do with why they chose the name, but SPREE was upset that the person critiquing them didn't know anything about them. Meanwhile, they did a show in LA and stayed with Harry Hay and John Burnside—founders of the Radical Faerie community, and longtime gay activists—and Harry threw a fit about the name controversy.

> MaxZine: Harry got so angry that we were considering changing the name. Like, irate. The way Harry could get. He was like "If you

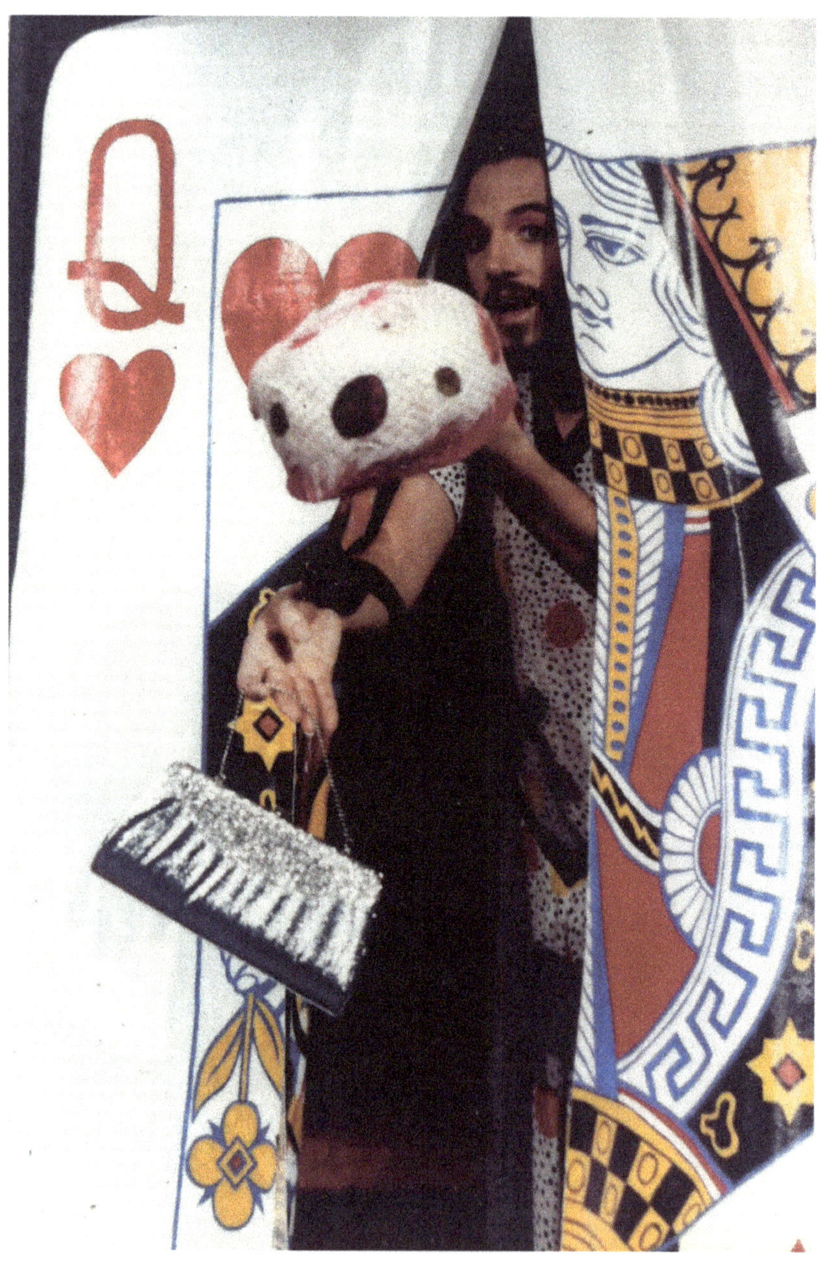

"Queens Are Wild" (EFP personal collection)

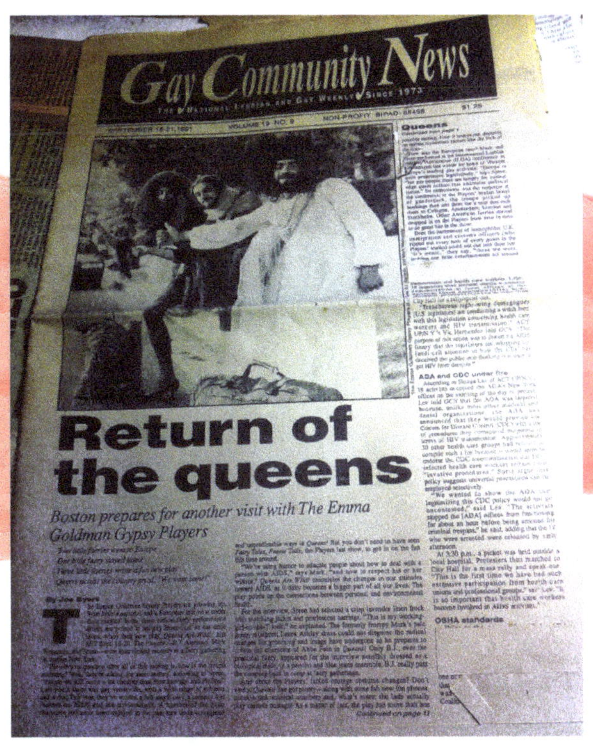

"Queens Are Wild" Gay Community News Article, 1991 (EFP personal collection)

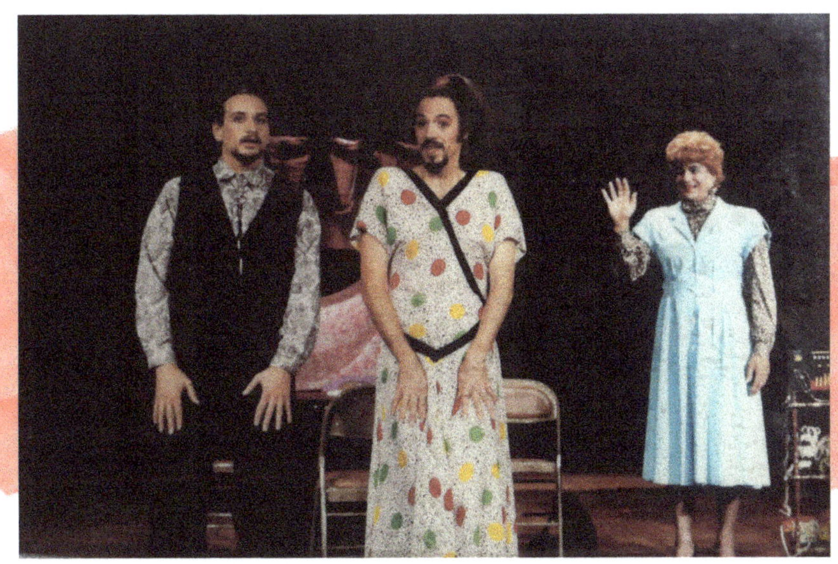

"Queens Are Wild" (B.J. Atanasco, SPREE, MaxZine) (EFP personal collection)

do that, I will have *no respect for you*. That is *wrong!* You have to keep this name!" And he's like "Let me tell you, back in the '20s or '30s I did theater with Will Geer and when we did this we called ourselves *gypsies*. That is a term of the stage and no one can tell you it's *not* a term of the stage!" His veins are popping out, and I'm like, Jesus, chill the fuck out, dude. We had really hard discussions about it.

In the end they changed their name for a few reasons: the critique of racism, the audience confusion about who Emma Goldman was, and MaxZine's growing concern that Emma Goldman's radical legacy was being commodified in a way he didn't want to participate in. They took the acronym EGGPLANT from "Emma Goldman Gypsy Players Annual National Tour" and became the Eggplant Faerie Players in 1991.

EGGPLANT FAERIE PLAYERS TOUR THROUGH THE 90s

On tour with *Queens Are Wild* in Europe, they connected with a Danish theater troupe active in the gay liberation movement in Denmark. MaxZine remembers that they were "these radical queer people who didn't just want civil rights but wanted to take on the whole patriarchal culture" and hearing stories about creative direct actions they had done, he felt like "oh my god, this is my people!" They made plans to collaborate and MaxZine and SPREE were going to move to Denmark, but their plans were tragically interrupted.

MaxZine: We had an amazing director lined up there and everything. There's a lot more support for the arts in Denmark than there was in the United States, or is now. So, it all was falling into place, except that then a lot of people got AIDS, or had AIDS and died, and the whole project fell apart.

I was lost, didn't know what to do with myself, and really sad to see these friends get sick and die. And also, because our theater project with all the funding we were planning on getting fell apart, I needed to earn some money. I came back to the USA to earn money … and then kind of realized that I was really burned out from living on the road so much, performing, and also having so many friends die.[105]

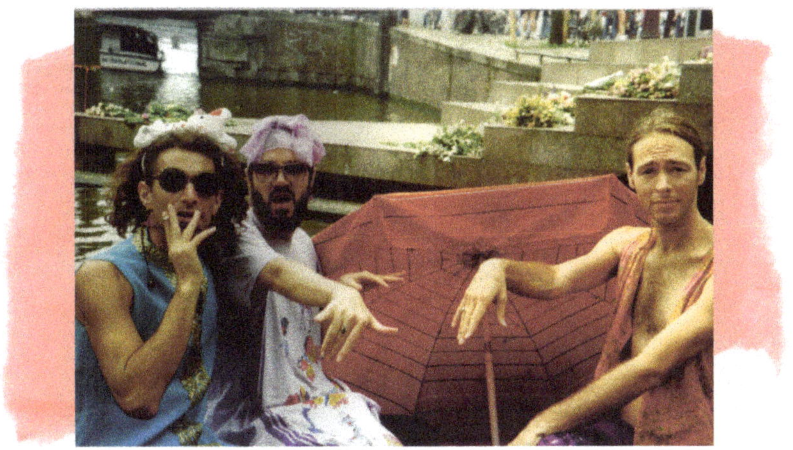

Traveling in Amsterdam (Sandor, SPREE, Michael Todd)
(EFP personal collection)

SPREE stayed on in Amsterdam in 1992, but MaxZine went back to Ann Arbor and started a gay newspaper called *Between the Lines*. When MaxZine made a trip to visit a Tennessee Faerie sanctuary in the fall of 1993, he heard from resident Sandor Katz (aka Sandy, Sandorfag, and Sandorkraut) about a newly forming queer arts community starting nearby—Idyll Dandy Arts (IDA)—and decided to move there. When MaxZine and Sandy went to visit SPREE in Amsterdam, Sandy decided

---

105 From an interview with MaxZine Weinstein posted on blog "Sharing & Caring" by David Sheen.

to stay longer to hang out with friends in Berlin so SPREE used Sandy's return ticket to come back to IDA with MaxZine.

Reunited at IDA, MaxZine and SPREE decided to restart the Eggplant Faerie Players. In the summer of 1994, with their fellow IDA residents and other friends from neighboring faerie communities, they wrote and toured a show called *Swishing Channels*. The show sets up a parody TV-land called the Pink Triangle Television Network. Skits include commercials for Queerios cereal, He/She's Harvey Milk Chocolate, Rainbow Shoes, and a condom recycling factory. The audience meets a psychic channeler named Crystal Debris (played by SPREE) who has her own Channel Surfing Channel, and fellow IDA resident Ha![106] performed a character named Rosie Meadows who was a star of the design channel. The *Swishing Channels* plot revolves around a gay man who falls in love with a virtual reality sex partner.

"Gay channel surfing and satire." Michigan Daily. 11/16/94.

The five [touring performers] claim that *Swishing Channels* will offend you: "I'm offended by it and I'm even in it," SPREE admitted. "But you're laughing at the next thing before you realize you're offended by the last," he added. EGGPLANT always finds the reactions of the audience interesting. MaxZine noted, "It must do some weird emotional number (to the audience) to be offended and laughing at the same time." The show, of course, is intentionally and necessarily offensive in order to depict the difficult issues facing the GLBi community. "Sometimes it is hard to tell if we are more offensive than reality, or if it is the other way around," SPREE commented. Perhaps by satirizing reality, EGGPLANT tried to gain a better grasp of it, in order to discover what needs to be changed.

---

106 Ha! is intentionally spelled with exclamation point included.

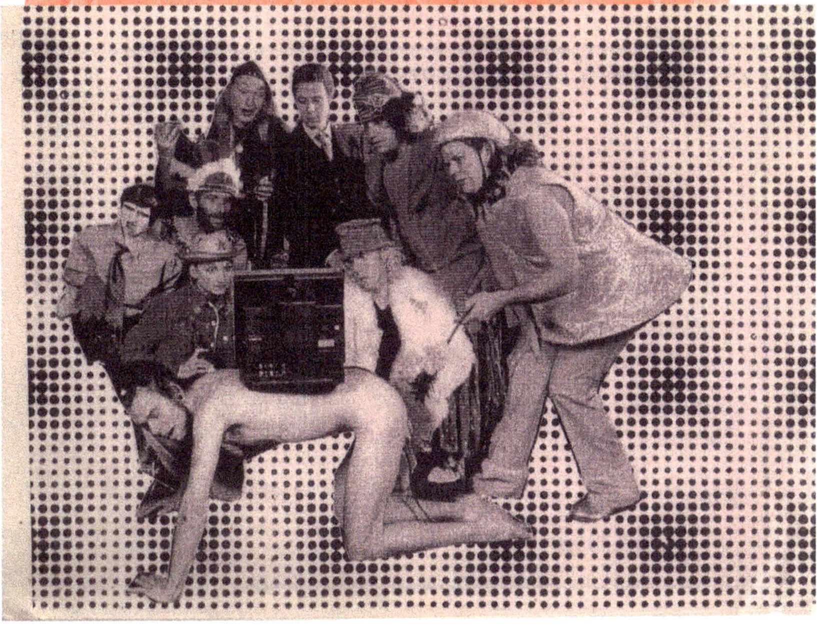

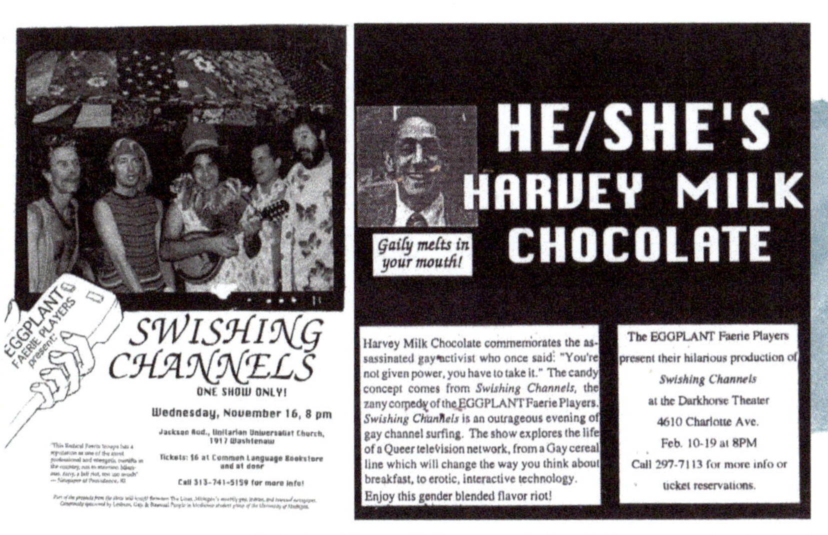

"Swishing Channels" Promo Image (EFP personal collection)

"Swishing Channels" Poster and Flyer (EFP personal collection)

The year was 1995 when these rural queers envisioned a capitalist media co-optation of gay culture, mixed up with the very beginnings of the Internet as we now know it. Looking back, Leopard—a Short Mountain member of the Eggplant Faerie Players—called it "a premonition show about gay consumerism before gay consumerism actually happened." Sandy describes it as "these two couch potato characters fantasizing about an all gay TV network, just a minute before that actually happened."

That same year, while on tour with *Swishing Channels*, at the Trumbullplex theater in Detroit, SPREE was putting on makeup and noticed a lesion on her eyelid, and then one between her toes. She told MaxZine she thought she had Kaposi's sarcoma (KS), an AIDS-associated opportunistic infection. SPREE got the run-around from doctors who told her first that she had an eyelid bruise and a fungus between her toes, then that she had syphilis. Back in Tennessee, she finally got a diagnosis of KS, but not before jumping through outrageous hoops to get healthcare benefits covered through the state's Tenn-Care program. SPREE almost died of AIDS in 1996, but she lived just long enough to be pulled back from the brink by the new treatment option of protease inhibitors.[107]

SPREE went on Norvir,[108] a brand-new protease inhibitor AIDS medication which was later used as part of a combination therapy (or "cocktail"), but as one of the earliest users, she took it as a mono-therapy.

SPREE: *Oh my god* it made me *sick as a dog*. I threw up everything I ate for three weeks. I was laying in the bed in the back house and they were just all expecting me to die any day. One morning I woke up and I was lying there in bed and I had had these visions, or visitations, from celestial somethings—or some aliens. Call them whatever you want, but they were like, "Just come with us, you can get out of your body, you don't have to be in pain

---

107 A medical advance that ACT UP can take a lot of credit for, as documented in the recent film *How to Survive a Plague* and elsewhere.
108 Norvir is the brand name, Ritonavir is the generic drug name.

anymore, you don't have to suffer, just let go and come with us," and I was like *nope!* I'm not done here. I'm not finished. And as tempting as it was to just go, "Okay!" I said *girl* if you throw up everything you eat, day after day, your body is not going to get any nourishment or nutrition or anything like that. And I got up weak as could be at six in the morning, and you know I'm *not seen* at six o'clock in the morning. And walked from the back house to the front house and said "I am going to cook myself breakfast." And this other person who saw me and almost had a heart attack was like, "What are you doing?" And I said I'm going to cook myself breakfast. And they're like, "Oh, do you want me to help you?" And I'm like, "Nope. It's very important, I have to do it myself." And then I made myself eggs and toast and a very nice little breakfast and I sat down and said "Now you are going to eat this and you are not going to throw it up." And I ate it and I just started to get better and better and better and better and better.

Reading through the *Radical Faerie Digest* archives, I came across a two-page piece in the Summer 1996 Issue: "Mad Dr. Science, Trying Not To Be Bitter, Leaving Loved: SPREE Vance Reflects on the Emotional Rollercoaster of Living with AIDS." In this interview, which was conducted by Sandy sitting under the covers in bed with SPREE, she reflects on reentering the land of the living after she had made peace with her impending death. She's uneasy—she doesn't know if her improved health will last. I had read SPREE's ACT UP Oral History interview, and she told me about the experience in our interview as well, but I was still somehow unprepared for the vulnerability of this in-the-moment interview that documents the exact end of the Plague Years in the voice of one person who just barely made it out alive and doesn't know what the future will hold.

Imagine suddenly lesions start popping out on you, and then you live your life a year and a half getting more of them, and them getting bigger. So you start, in your mind, living your life thinking

> you're going along a certain path, that indeed you are heading to-
> ward transformation. You are going to go somewhere else. You
> might have to leave this body and this realm. Then along comes
> mad Dr. Science with his magic pill and says, "Look, all you have
> to do is take this poison, and maybe you don't have to die, maybe
> you will get better," when I have been living my life the last year
> and a half thinking I am not going to get better. But now I have
> this new chance. Your new lease on life. Just take our poison and
> you can zap that virus right out of your body. So yeah, it totally
> fucks with your head. Perhaps the path I have been on is not that
> path at all, that you can take a side detour and be around for an-
> other, like, six months or two years or ten years—or what if the
> lesions all go away and I am all better, wouldn't that be great. But
> what if in six months my body is resistant to the protease inhib-
> itors...[109]

SPREE started to get better, but she also got really manic. It turned out that you weren't supposed to take the antidepressant drug Paxil with Norvir, but it was so new that her doctor didn't catch that interaction detail. Her body was flooded with serotonin and she had what she "fondly refers to as a meltdown" that led to hospitalization in a Nash-ville psychiatric ward.

SPREE processed these experiences through theater. At first, she want-ed to do a production of her friend Michael Smith's play *Person Livid with AIDS*. Smith had ended his life after a succession of AIDS-related hospitalizations, and SPREE wanted to get a script or tape of his show but she couldn't track down a copy despite trying many avenues. Finally MaxZine said to SPREE, "Well why don't you just do your own story. Be-cause, you've been through so much now that *you* could be the person livid with AIDS."

109 "Mad Dr. Science, Trying Not To Be Bitter, Leaving Loved: SPREE Vance Reflects on the Emotional Rollercoaster of Living with AIDS. As told to Sandorfag and transcribed by Susan Stoddard." *Radical Faerie Digest*, Summer 1996 (#86, Regenerating Fleeting Dhar-mas): 42-43.

In putting the pieces back together, SPREE reclaimed her agency. She remixed her own history, using parts of her story that were fragmented by her traumatic illness and mental health crisis, weaving them in with old and new performance pieces from the Eggplant Faerie Player collection.

The Eggplant Faeries put on a group show centered on SPREE's story at the Dark Horse Theater in Nashville and then toured throughout the South. The show opens in darkness with the voices of cast members singing a number of children's songs re-written to be about AIDS. Lights up on SPREE, sitting center stage in the wheelchair she had used during her increasing illness. MaxZine puts a hat on SPREE and says, "Tag, you're it." SPREE looks eerie, sort of frozen, but her eyes move back and forth dramatically. Finally she says:

> Alright, Mr. DeMille, I'm ready for my close up. Norma Desmond, this is your life. No, wait a minute, stop the tape! Stop, rewind, back up! That's not what this is at all. This isn't even "Gloria Swanson, this is *your* life." This is supposed to be "*SPREE*, this is your life." Oh, well, then in that case—alright, Mr. DeMille, I'm ready for my tap dance.
>
> *[Tap dances while saying:]* Hello everybody, my name's SPREE! What's yours?
>
> *[Finishes dancing:]* And that on feet that had the lesions radiated off of them, thank you very much!

From her chair, SPREE tells her story: working at the National AIDS Hotline, getting overwhelmed by losing so many people, testing positive, having to jump through ridiculous hoops to access treatment, and her experience finally getting on the protease inhibitors and having a mental breakdown. Throughout this retelling, skits and song-and-dance interludes theatrically illuminate the story.

SPREE's classic character Barbara Broadcast tells her hilarious tales of calls to the AIDS hotline with a bevy of fancy queers *kibitzing* on phones behind her. Then SPREE does an onstage outfit change to become R.J. Sneevely while introducing Ha! as Rosie Meadows, ready to interview Sneevely about his condom recycling factory.

In the original play, Michael Smith performed an imagined confrontation with a Canadian Member of Parliament, taking off all his clothes and showing his KS lesions, saying to the MP: "Look at me, look at my body, I am a person livid with AIDS." SPREE remembers that Smith was using the "anger" definition of livid, but when she looked up the word in the Merriam-Webster dictionary, she was amazed to find that the first definition of "livid" is "discolored by bruising: black-and-blue."[110]

In the Eggplant Faerie Player show, Dashboard jumps up from the audience wearing a "FIGHT AIDS NOT ARABS" T-shirt and interrupts the condom recycling factory skit, starting the following dialogue:

> Dashboard: Stop the show! This wasn't livid; this was funny. It was humorous but it wasn't livid. What happened to outrage? What happened to fury? What happened to external manifestation of internal conflict projected on individuals and institutions in positions of power and authority? What happened to anger!
>
> SPREE: [*Explains about the bruise definition of livid, lifts her shirt to show her KS lesions, then*] I am a person livid with AIDS, get it? And if I happen to think that humor is a good way of dealing with this epidemic or pandemic or whatever you want to call it, then so be it!
>
> Dashboard: [*Getting more and more angry*] Well that's just not good enough. People that I love died and it doesn't matter how much I care for them, how much I cry. It doesn't matter if I'm ready

---

110 http://www.merriam-webster.com/dictionary/livid.

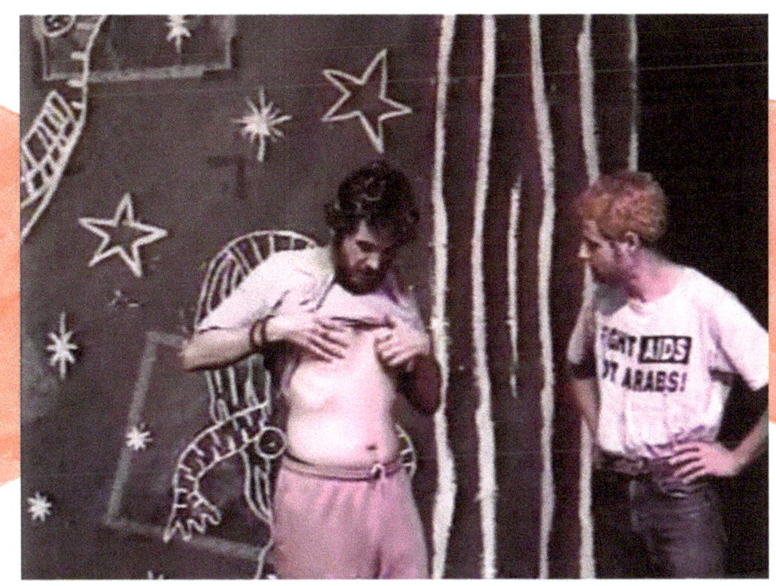

"Person Livid With AIDS," SPREE explains "livid" definition to Dashboard
(Video screenshot by author)

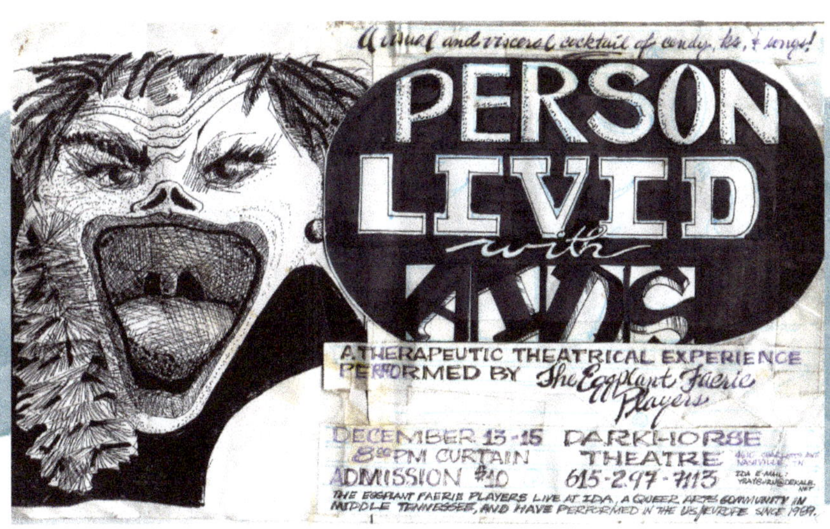

"Person Livid With AIDS" Poster, 1996 (EFP personal collection)

for them to go or not, they die and there is nothing that I can do and it just makes me want to throw a brick at some government office or kill Jesse Helms or something. Ahhhhh! [*Screams his way off the stage.*]

SPREE: Well you go, girl, you go!

Red Ribbon: [*Walks timidly across the stage, looking scared*] Please stop all the shouting, open yourself up to the white light. AIDS is about feeling good, cause you know that someone somewhere is doing something for you.

SPREE: Oh yes, right, it's about red ribbons and AIDS merchandising and things like that, and about New Age and learning to heal ourselves and Louise Hay and getting in touch with our inner virus and learning to love the virus within and that sort of thing.

This leads into SPREE's scene as New Age character Crystal Debris, a tongue-in-cheek character used to critique those who encouraged people with HIV/AIDS to simply use positive thinking to heal themselves. Crystal explains how she came to have psychic powers and encourages viewers to buy her new book *How to Impress Your Immune System*.

[The book] is for our dear viewers out there who are immune-impaired. Through the knowledge and information in my book you will be able to learn how to impress your own immune system so much that you will then be able to impress others with it. Now, we try to impress others with our looks, our talents, our knowledge, our personalities. Why not our immune systems? And think about it folks, if you are so impressed with your own immune system that you are able to impress others with it, then there is just no possible way that it could be repressed, oppressed, suppressed, or depressed.

As the show continues, SPREE tells of the outrageous barriers to competent medical care that she faced. Even despite being an ACT UP activist, an information specialist with the AIDS Hotline, and having a friend who worked at the Center for Disease Control, the layers of catch-22 drama she had to deal with are exhausting to recount. Finally, she calls in her friends to help her, and they do a fabulous musical clowning number called the "Tenn-Care Shuffle."

The show became a group-production, with a dozen people involved in writing and performing numbers, including a rewrite of the classic Passover song *"Chad Gad'ya,"* in which Dashboard—as the Angel of Death—recounts a string of HIV-transmission methods in which both none and all are innocent.

But the group had moved in a different direction than SPREE envisioned for this show focused on her experience. She'd come to the group with a vision of performing as a teacher, telling the school children about A-I-D-S and going into a long string of wordplay. Some of that initial monologue about letters, words, and sign language made it into the first part of the show, but the group didn't support her doing the full scene she envisioned, and people starting adding their own scenes. SPREE ended up writing her frustration about loss of control over her own story into the play, as well.

> SPREE: Finally I just stand up out of my wheelchair and go, "Wait a minute! That's not how it really happened! This is *my* story!"
>
> Q: So you put that process in the show?
>
> S: Yeah, when I got to the point where I said, "You're telling this out of order, this is wrong, this is not the way that it happened. First this happened and then this happened and then I had a breakdown." And then I reenacted the breakdown.
>
> Q: Was it cathartic?

S: Oh sure, yes, oh definitely. That's why I was doing it, to let it go and give it back out to the universe and hopefully educate some people.

"Play vividly shows life of AIDS patient" THE TENNESSEAN. 9/14/1996

Person Livid With AIDS, tonight and tomorrow at Darkhorse Theater, isn't for the squeamish. But if you want to know how a person lives with AIDS and what he encounters in the process, the Eggplant Faerie Players will turn that livid into vivid as you watch and empathize. There's no moralizing about getting infected—or avoiding infection. It's about "empowerment, community, friends," as lead actor SPREE dramatizes his seven years with HIV and two years with AIDS in theatrical, often humorous, sketches. A professional actor with a quick wit, he founded the performing company, which has toured in the United States and Europe, and wrote this comedy drama in collaboration with his eleven fellow actors. He also calls upon his New York experience as a National AIDS Hotline counselor for some of his material; the silly questions he was asked make viewers squirm. The show is based on his actual experience as an AIDS patient, a gay man and a transvestite who is quite beautiful, beard notwithstanding, in his female apparel. His recital of the red tape in getting attention when you're uninsured and spanning the bureaucracy of Tenn-Care, Blue Cross-Blue Shield, inattentive medical personnel and the onslaught of experimental medications make for devastating humor. SPREE found that when he was diagnosed he couldn't take what he'd been dishing out on the hot-line, "You play mind games then," he says, "you rearrange reality." His hallucinating in the hospital is mind-boggling to a viewer who feels he, too, is boxed in in that lonely, unattended space. SPREE's alternate ego, Barbara Broadcast of *Swishing Channels*, has a funny sketch that must be seen to be believed, and is later castigated by an angry youth who shouts that the script is not livid, "it's stupid," until SPREE explains that "livid" means bruised and that those with AIDS suffer such skin spots. Music played on accordion, guitar, and mandolin intensifies the mood of anger and melancholy, of tenderness and raunchiness, and even of hope in this astonishing work.

Also in 1997, a gathering at IDA called "Night of 1000 Stars" offers another example of the Eggplant Faerie Players and friends using performance and playfulness to respond to HIV/AIDS in their intimate community and the local area. After digitizing a number of MaxZine and SPREE's VHS and Hi-8 tapes, I was able to watch a video of the 1997 "Night of 1000 Stars" gathering, and it was a great thrill to witness the riotous, brilliant creative chaos of this event. The video opens with a runway walk-off where each partier is announced and promenades to the applause of the crowd. SPREE is the last one out, her arrival hyped by a Faerie (Keer) in suit and tie drag talking into a giant cardboard cell phone: "She's on her way! She's almost here!" After a dramatic entrance, SPREE introduces the party, explaining that it's a fundraiser for both IDA and the local ("non-Faerie") HIV/AIDS support group. The acreage of IDA had been turned into a giant board game and MaxZine is transformed into a giant board game-spinner, with a big pink triangle strap-on that lands on different game options with each spin.

After much running around and game-playing, the party regroups at the porch of the back house for another speech by SPREE, who explains that one year ago, on May 11, 1996, she suddenly decided it was Magic Day. That day she had asked each person three questions: Do you believe in faeries? Do you believe in magic? Do you believe in the power of your heart to change the world? She envisioned that one year later they would hold the Night of 1000 Stars. She doesn't say this in the video, but on Magic Day, 1996, SPREE didn't really know if she'd be alive a year later—and here she is, manifesting her Magic Day vision. In the video, the camera person holds a pink star bubble-blowing wand in front of the camera so that in the camera's frame, SPREE is surrounded by the star. It's a perfect moment. She is a star. We are all stars. The power of our magic hearts to change the world.

Soon after the *Person Livid with AIDS* tour, the 1997 Southeast Gay and Lesbian Student Conference was held at Middle Tennessee State University [MTSU] in Murfreesboro, Tennessee—about an hour from IDA—

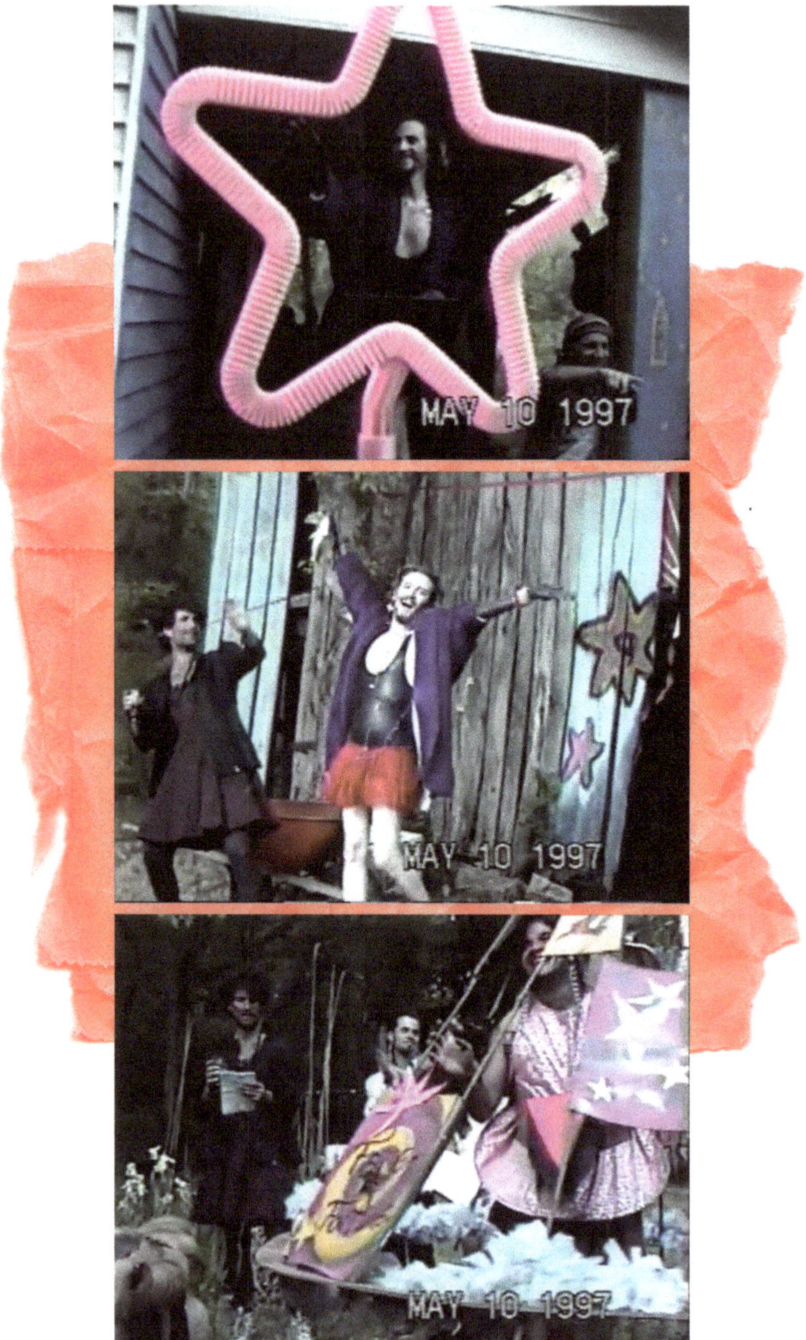

Magic Day, May 10 1997 (Video screenshots by author)

and the Eggplant Faerie Players were invited to perform. They made a new show for the event: "45 minutes of the most absurd, offensive stuff we could come up with." There were Christian Right protests of the gathering, claiming that gays want to seduce and recruit children, and the MTSU President was on record with anti-gay statements. In response, the Eggplant Faerie Players wrote a revenge-fantasy play about kidnapping the MTSU President and raping and reprogramming him into homosexuality, a spin on "ex-gay" brainwashing programs. It sounds disturbing, but it was played with goofy camp that apparently made the whole thing too silly to successfully offend. In the show, the organization Faggots United In Contextual Karmic Determination Up-root Power (FUCKD UP) kidnapped the President, as played by Ha!, and the instrument of violation used on the president was a drill-dildo ("dril-do") operated by a nine-year-old girl! The reprogramming consisted of demanding that the president choose between a series of options such as: "Iceberg lettuce or Belgian endives?!" and he gets in trouble every time he chooses the straight option. This ends up turning the president into a sex-crazed monster-dominatrix who out-gays all the members of FUCKD UP. The goal was to be totally outrageous, but in the end it may have been so out-there that the audience had lots of fun but didn't fully "get it" enough to be offended. Leopard remembers that he did a monologue intended as a parody piece about ten reasons gay people should assimilate, but the audience likely took it as a serious piece: "I think there was, in that show in particular, a sort of disconnect between us as performers and the audience. I don't think they really got it. Or we didn't really want to be got—we wanted to be punky, bratty performers on some level."

I was shocked to hear a child had been involved in the show in this way, but I appreciated MaxZine's writing about the political commitment behind that decision:

> If we want our theatrical endeavors to encourage social change, we need to accept change in our community as well. We also

need to nourish the potential within the community members. A nine-year-old girl from Maine, who occasionally visits here with her dad, got involved in a performance we did for a gay and lesbian student activists conference. Part of our anarchistic theatrical process is that we each decide what roles we want to do. And so, she happily cast herself into a wild sex scene in the play. We mature adults had no problem with her in that role. We did realize that other mature adults might be upset with a young child in an S&M skit, but it was her decision and everyone respected it. The show (and especially that particular skit) were a hit, and students still talk about it to this day. Political theater lives. Addressing social ills with a clever wink and an irreverent laugh is an old tradition of which we are proud to be a part. Yet, our theater is not just a response to the painful political reality around us. What we do on stage is a reflection of how we choose to live our lives. Our theatrical end-result is a testimony to the process that produced it. It's created by consensus, is empowering, and thrives in community.[111]

This is a great example of the strategies of rehearsing resistance and dazzle camouflage coming together. In the making of this show, the performers practiced collective decision-making and got to decide for themselves what role they wanted in their play and in the imagined liberation movement. And, at the same time, the use of the ridiculous as dazzle camouflage comes into play as a nine-year-old girl using a "drildo" brings surprise and humor to a scene that might otherwise have pushed more threatening buttons.

The MTSU show was a hastily brainstormed production, but the Eggplant Faerie Players took elements from it and created a new full show, *Dial M for Mothership*. This new show replaced the MTSU President with the Pope, partly because a number of the Eggplant Faerie Players were

---

111 MaxZine Weinstein, "Radical Faerie Activism. Part Two of Two." *AGENDA: Monthly Independent News and Culture around Ann Arbor*, March 1999.

recovering Catholics and Ha! especially was always talking about wanting to kidnap the Pope. It was also a response to all the hubbub about the impending millennium. A cult called Heaven's Gate had committed mass suicide in March 1997, while the Eggplant Faerie Players were writing the show. Heaven's Gate had believed that the Hale-Bopp comet was tailed by an alien spacecraft and they would be able to join with the aliens after death.

> TomFoolery: And then we took that and said, well let's do it, and it's all the people who've died of AIDS and their energy is fueling this Mothership that's gonna bring—
>
> Dashboard: Peace and harmony. Using a lot of our general themes, we were looking at this convergence of all those insane groups as they're dealing with the approaching millennia. You get the Catholic church, you get all those gay activists who are kind of going crazy, you get the Hale-Bopp Pharmaceuticals, who was the pharmaceuticals company who's trying to figure out how to create the next generation of drugs. And then you had the Queen of the Mothership and her two evil advisors, who are trying to take over the Mothership. It all kind of fell out.
>
> T: And meanwhile, she's bringing Peace with her, this diva.
>
> D: Right, which is also this whole parody about the idea that the millennium would bring peace as much as bring disaster.

In the summer of 1998, a few months after the *Mothership* tour ended, Dashboard, MaxZine, and Jonas (aka Peter Panzy—another Radical Faerie performer friend from New York) planned a trip to Israel. MaxZine didn't want to go Israel without bringing a show, and that's how *Next Year in Sodom* was born—"an irreverent satire of Jewish tradition, religion, and politics in the holy land."

MaxZine had grown up in a Jewish family, and the Eggplant Faerie Players had always written Jewish mothers, Yiddish-style jokes, and other Jewish culture into their shows, but it was Dashboard—another key Eggplant Faerie Player—who brought Israeli politics to the group.

Dashboard was born in Jerusalem and grew up in a secular family that wasn't political, but he moved toward the Left at a young age. Dashboard was a seventeen-year-old exchange student in upstate New York in 1982 when Israel invaded Lebanon, and he was horrified by revelations of the Sabra and Shatila massacres.[112] Returning to Israel, he gravitated toward his Leftist friends who identified as non-Zionist. Dashboard joined the pacifist movement, and at eighteen, he refused to join the Israeli military—eventually negotiating to accept a desk job instead of a combat position. After a period living in a kibbutz, Dashboard moved to New York in 1990. There, he quickly got involved with the Radical Faeries and ACT UP NY, and eventually moved to a Faerie sanctuary in Tennessee. He goes back to Israel every year to visit family and friends.

With *Next Year in Sodom*, the Eggplant Faerie Players turned their gaze to international politics on a new level. Perhaps the evolution of the AIDS crisis prompted by protease inhibitors made it possible to shift AIDS slightly away from the center of their theatrical stage, making room for other politics to step farther forward into the spotlights. Still, while the subject matter was serious, the Eggplant Faerie writing process was as slapdash and playful as usual—Dashboard and MaxZine brainstormed most of the plot at a Willie Nelson concert.

The person who produced them in Israel got their show a two-page spread in the culture section of the leading Israeli daily paper—the article called them "Gay Kibbutzniks." Because of the article, they were

---

112 A massacre of Palestinian and Lebanese Shia refugees living in the Sabra and Shatila refugee camps in West Beirut, Lebanon following the Israeli invasion of Lebanon. The violence was carried out by a Lebanese Christian militia, but a UN commission and an internal Israeli investigation held the Israeli Defense Forces responsible for allowing the massacre without intervening.

invited to do a segment on a the television show *Erev Chadash*, and "everyone in Israel saw it." MaxZine wrote about the experience:

> When a national news magazine television show invited us to perform a scene from the play, we chose a love scene between Moses and the Pharaoh. We wanted to send a message that everything is possible, including lewd historical interpretations. So, we went to the studio, put on make-up, wigs, and costumes, and paraded down the long hallway in scantily clad outfits. We don't know what those in the studio (including cameramen with yarmulkes, the Mayor of Tel Aviv, the cabinet minister) thought when they saw us performing the scene. But a few days later we knew we had successfully slaughtered a sacred cow. Two young men approached us on the street to tell us that they had seen us on TV and encouraged us to "keep fucking with the world." With public support for radical political theater lower than low, these kinds of supportive comments give us the energy to continue creating and performing.[113]

During their time in Israel, The Eggplant Faeries visited a peace camp in support of Bedouins who were being forcibly displaced from their land by Jewish condominium construction. At the peace camp, they met Palestinians who invited them to their home for lunch and told them about the horrors of the Israeli brutality. When the Eggplant Faeries told their Israeli friends about what they'd learned, their friends wouldn't hear it. Dashboard remembers:

> Certain aspects of [our trip to Israel] were very traumatic. Just being exposed to the occupation in a much more visceral way than obviously MaxZine or Jonas had ever seen, and even for me kind of seeing it through their eyes, but also dealing with friends we were hanging out with who were totally loving everything we were doing but the minute we got into that kind of politics got

---

113 Weinstein,"Radical Faerie Activism. Part Two of Two."

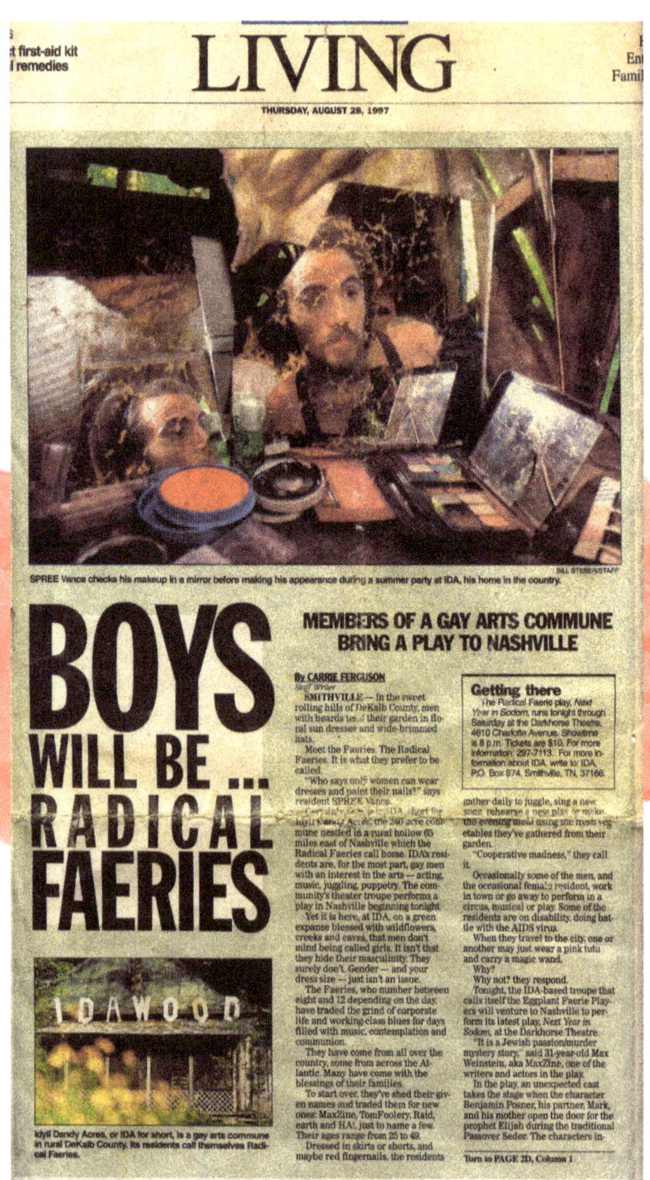

LIVING

THURSDAY, AUGUST 28, 1997

SPREE Vance checks his makeup in a mirror before making his appearance during a summer party at IDA, his home in the country.

BOYS
WILL BE ...
RADICAL
FAERIES

Idyll Dandy Acres, or IDA for short, is a gay arts commune in rural DeKalb County. Its residents call themselves Radical Faeries.

MEMBERS OF A GAY ARTS COMMUNE BRING A PLAY TO NASHVILLE

By CARRIE FERGUSON
Staff Writer

SMITHVILLE — In the sweet rolling hills of DeKalb County, men with beards tend their garden in floral sun dresses and wide-brimmed hats.

Meet the Faeries. The Radical Faeries. It is what they prefer to be called.

"Who says only women can wear dresses and paint their nails?" says resident SPREE Vance.

Certainly not is in IDA, short for Idyll Dandy Acres, the 240-acre commune nestled in a rural hollow 65 miles east of Nashville which the Radical Faeries call home. IDA's residents are, for the most part, gay men with an interest in the arts — acting, music, juggling, puppetry. The community's theater troupe performs a play in Nashville beginning tonight.

Yet it is here, at IDA, on a green expanse blessed with wildflowers, creeks and caves, that men don't mind being called girls. It isn't that they hide their masculinity. They surely don't. Gender — and your dress size — just isn't an issue.

The Faeries, who number between eight and 12 depending on the day, have traded the grind of corporate life and working-class blues for days filled with music, contemplation and communion.

They have come from all over the country, some from across the Atlantic. Many have come with the blessings of their families.

To start over, they've shed their given names and traded them for new ones: MaxZine, TomFoolery, Raid, earth and HA!, just to name a few. Their ages range from 25 to 49.

Dressed in skirts or shorts, and maybe red fingernails, the residents gather daily to juggle, sing a new song, rehearse a new play or make the evening meal using the fresh vegetables they've gathered from their garden.

"Cooperative madness," they call it.

Occasionally some of the men, and the occasional female resident, work in town or go away to perform in a circus, musical or play. Some of the residents are on disability, doing battle with the AIDS virus.

When they travel to the city, one or another may just wear a pink tutu and carry a magic wand.

Why?

Why not? they respond.

Tonight, the IDA-based troupe that calls itself the Eggplant Faerie Players will venture to Nashville to perform its latest play, *Next Year in Sodom*, at the Darkhorse Theatre.

"It is a Jewish passion/murder mystery story," said 31-year-old Max Weinstein, aka MaxZine, one of the writers and actors in the play.

In the play, an unexpected cast takes the stage when the character Benjamin Posner, his partner, Mark, and his mother open the door for the prophet Elijah during the traditional Passover Seder. The characters in-

Turn to PAGE 2D, Column 1

Getting there

The Radical Faerie play, *Next Year in Sodom*, runs tonight through Saturday at the Darkhorse Theatre, 4610 Charlotte Avenue. Showtime is 8 p.m. Tickets are $10. For more information: 297-7113. For more information about IDA, write to: IDA, P.O. Box 874, Smithville, TN, 37166.

"Next Year in Sodom," 1997 feature article (EFP personal collection)

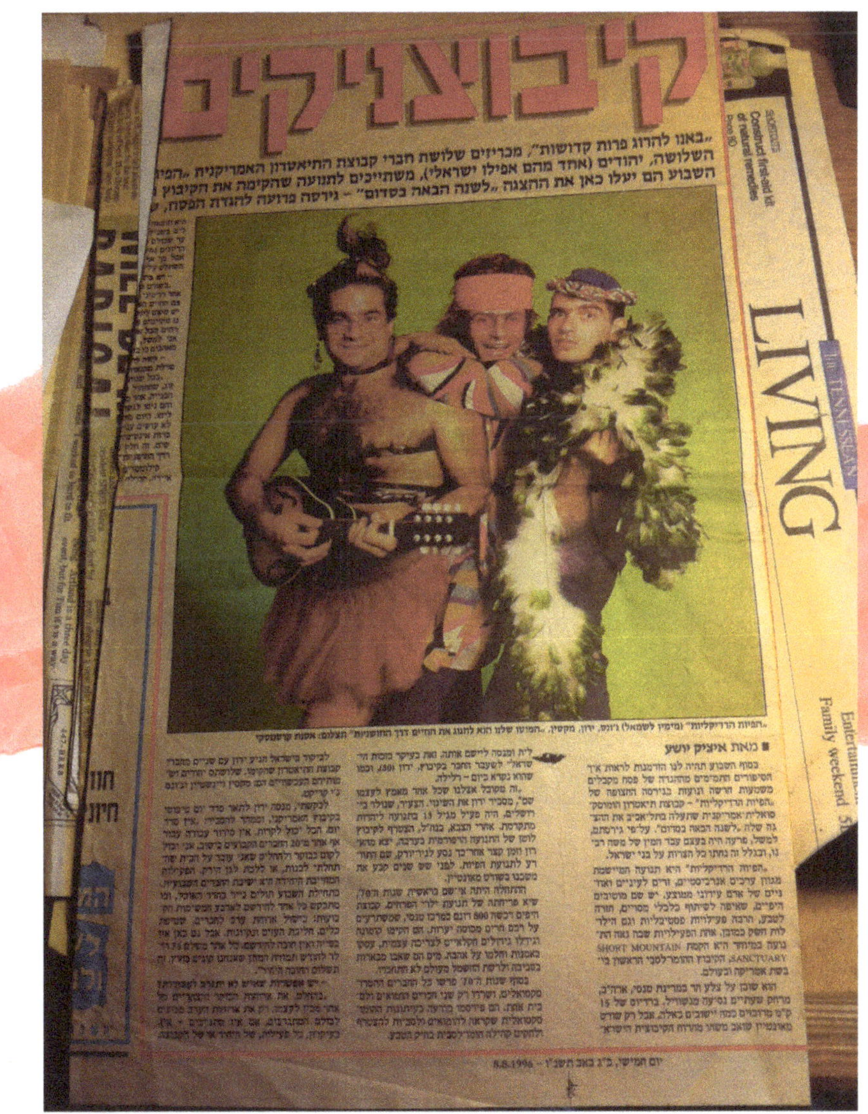

"Next Year in Sodom," 1997 Israeli feature article (EFP personal collection)

kind of fascistic, really. So we wrote [a new] skit as an emotional catharsis of this and added it to the play.

They added a scene about gay lovers who are Israeli and Palestinian. In this scene, the lovers are interviewed by Butch Weiner of the Gay News Network (GNN), and we learn that each of their family members have caused destruction in the others' lives, in an escalating conflict. The lovers argue about it, refusing to let the other take the blame for the situation.

Palestinian: But you have to understand that the Jews had nowhere to go after the Holocaust. Israel was the natural choice.

Israeli: With all due respect to the Holocaust, even before the Holocaust, Jews were immigrating to Palestine.

P: Well, Israel was promised to your people by God.

I: But that does not excuse stealing lands from the Palestinians who lived there peacefully long before we took it over.

P: You did not take it over. You reclaimed it. You were returning to your homeland.

I: We stole it from your people.

P: My people could always go to any of the many Arab countries throughout the Middle East.

I: That is a very limited view of the situation, and a very poor excuse for ruthlessly turning millions of Palestinians into refugees.[114]

---

114 Nettles, "Eggplant Faerie Players Profile," 28.

This scene was written two years before the outbreak of the Second Intifada (Palestinian uprising), and seven years before the launch of the Palestinian Boycott, Divestment, Sanctions (BDS) Movement. Looking at the dialogue more than fifteen years later, I could offer a critique that it sets up a sense of a "conflict" with two equivalent sides when in reality the violence, harm, and destruction caused by Israel's military aggression vastly outweighs that of the Palestinian resistance.[115] I also think that if this played today, the show would be criticized for putting Zionist talking points into the Palestinian character's mouth. But I also see a theatrical strategy here—a way to get audiences to hear the lines that criticize Israel, because they are spoken by the Israeli character. Jewish voices are privileged in conversations about Israel—that's one reason why groups like New Jewish Agenda, Jews Against the Occupation, and Jewish Voice for Peace have organized to publicly challenge Israel *as Jews*. These groups also must be careful about overshadowing Palestinian voices and organizing in their use of this solidarity strategy, but it's a balancing act—silence is not the answer.

In the fall of 1998, The Eggplant Faeries (now with TomFoolery instead of Jonas) took the show on a US tour, including a run at Nashville's Dark Horse Theater. I asked the Eggplant Faeries about audience responses to this show, and they named a few experiences: a Jewish WWII veteran who saw the show in Nashville dressed in his military uniform and thanked the performers afterwards, and a Holocaust survivor who saw the show in New Mexico and was upset about airing Jewish dirty laundry in front of non-Jews. In Louisville, an Orthodox Jewish man told them "I was so worried when I heard about this play, that it was just going to be Israel-criticism, but it was so good to see how you introduced both sides of the story, and I loved the play and I loved the way that you presented a very balanced view on what's happening there." Dashboard remembers:

---

115 This critique relates to the BDS movement's opposition of "normalization" activities, which bring together Israeli and Palestinian individuals or organizations for dialogue or other collaborative activities without explicit commitment to expose and resist the Israeli occupation of Palestine and the oppression of Palestinian people.

I was like, "Did you just see the same play that we performed?" But I think that people see what they want to see and you know the Israeli-Palestinian skit is this absurd retelling of the conflict in this really kind of wacky, topsy-turvy way, and for him the topsy-turviness was enough for him to think that we were actually showing both sides, even though we weren't.

A Nashville woman they were friendly with didn't like the show's Rachel Bagelbaum character, complaining that she was a caricature of Zionism. The retelling of this criticism led to one of the funniest moments of my group interview with the EFPs.

MaxZine: She's like, "Not all Zionists are mindless supporters of Israel."

Dashboard: Even though *she* was.

M: And so she didn't like my character.

D: And the other thing she didn't like was that TomFoolery was juggling dicks, the scene where TomFoolery juggles dildos because—

M: —that's what TomFoolery *does*.

D: It's in his contract!

M: And he's still juggling those same dildos.

D: She came to me afterwards and said, "I love your play but I don't understand, why does he have to juggle dildos, why couldn't he juggle, I don't know—"

All: *Matzoh balls!*

The Israeli-Palestinian scene was created after the initial 1998 Israel tour, but in 2008 Dashboard attended the Queeruption (radical queer) gathering in Tel Aviv and performed the scene at the gathering's "No-Talent Show."

> Dashboard: It was a really empowering amazing experience to do that skit in front of an audience of Israelis and Palestinians and internationals, you know, all queer in Israel, and in Palestine, which was kind of closing the circle. And it ended up that it was exactly ten years since we did *Next Year in Sodom* in Israel for the first time, and it also ended up that there were two places where we performed *Next Year in Sodom* in Israel. One was a real theater and one was this gay nightclub. And Queeruption actually took place at that club, exactly ten years later. So here we are again—or me, doing this skit. I was kind of blown away. That was really beautiful. That was probably the most responsive audience that I've ever seen.

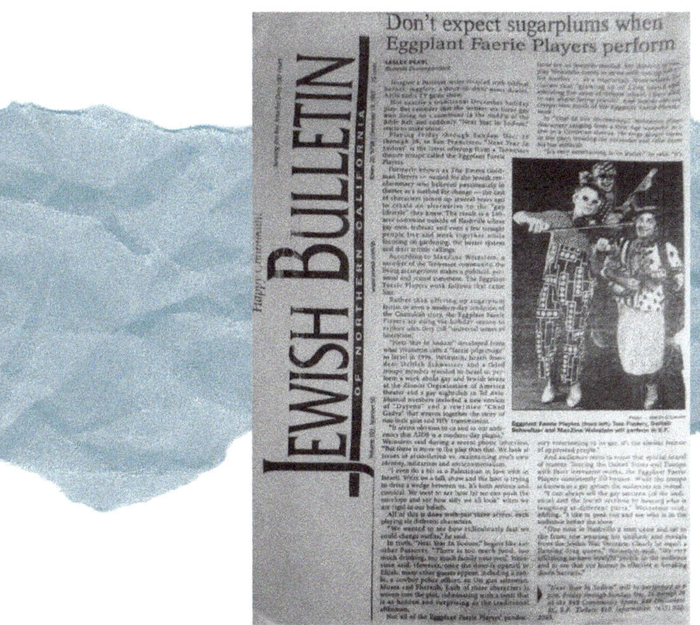

"Next Year in Sodom," 1997 Jewish Bulletin of Northern California article (EFP personal collection)

"Next Year in Ramah"[116]

In January '98, the Eggplant Faerie Players performed Next Year in Sodom to two sold-out audiences at a restaurant in the small town of Ramah, New Mexico. It was sponsored by the El Morro Arts Council.

Who would have thought "Next Year in Sodom" would play in Ramah, New Mexico, population 900, a small Mormon community abutted by the Navajo and Zuni Reservations. But the El Morro Arts Council (EMAAC) seized the opportunity of having the Eggplant Faerie Players in the area and presented two evenings of dinner theater at the Blue Corn Restaurant on the edge of town.

There had been some discussion of the play being too risqué for EMAAC to sponsor, would it shock the locals and have repercussions for our newly formed Arts Council? But deciding that the best art pushes boundaries, encourages dialog and wakes people up—we went ahead and quickly sold-out two performances.

The play was indeed a shocker, but it was witty, moving, poignant, funny, sometimes sad, silly and very, very, good. The play centered around a not-so-traditional Passover Seder shared by Benjamin Posner (TomFoolery), his lover Mark (MaxZine Weinstein) and Benjamin's mother Sea-weed (Delilah Deville). When they open the door for Elijah they invite in a whole cast of characters from Moses and his lover, Pharaoh, to a TV talk-show host interviewing a Palestinian/Jewish gay couple to a determined "Trees for Israel" saleswoman. All touching upon the theme of freedom amidst repression.

Most poignant was the beautifully written and performed music. Chad Gad'ya, a traditional Passover song, examined the question of blame versus victim in the transmission of HIV.

This fast-paced, irreverent romp brought peals of laughter from the audience and hours of discussion afterwards. The play was written and acted by three of the Eggplant Faerie Players, MaxZine Weinstein, TomFoolery, and the enormously talented Delilah Deville [aka Dashboard]. So, what's next year in Ramah?

---

116 Lisa De St. Croix, "Next Year in Ramah," *Zuni Mountain Sanctuary.*

At the end of the '90s, the Eggplant Faerie Players did a few different versions of variety-act shows including *Smoke Signals*, which included such hits as Lisa Lust singing "Girl with a Penis," "Herb Kind's Bong Show," juggling and fire spinning, strip teases, and many more musical numbers rewriting classic songs with lyrics about Nashville. *Smoke Signals* also included a long scene focused on retelling the story of Pomp Kersey, a local Civil War legend who lived near Short Mountain (home of many Eggplant Faerie Players) in the 1800s, and is actually buried on their land. Pomp Kersey was a soldier who fought in the Confederate army and then became an independent guerrilla soldier. There's an often-untold part of this Southern story: Kersey was said to have dressed in women's clothing to seduce Union soldiers and get secrets from them. Performing the Pomp Kersey story in Nashville, The Eggplant Faerie Players both reclaimed a piece of local dazzle camouflage history and critically engaged their region's relationship to Civil War history.

An Eggplant Faerie production of *Lysistrata* was a new model for the troupe—they took the ancient Greek play by Aristophanes and did the whole thing word-for-word. The premise of *Lysistrata* is women withholding sex unless the men stop fighting a war, and the Eggplant Faerie Player production queered the show with their outrageous drag as well as giant strap-ons that got bigger and bigger throughout the show as the men got progressively more frustrated without sex. SPREE remembers there was a review in the paper that said "If Aristophanes hadn't written *Lysistrata*, the Eggplant Faerie Players would have."

PROTEST PERFORMANCE

The Eggplant Faerie Player performance style draws heavily from street theater and direct action protests, a style MaxZine learned from Ann Arbor's Pinkerton Theater Group, and then evolved within ACT UP and other activist groups. What does dazzle camouflage look like when The Eggplant Faeries step out of touring specific productions, and apply their performative methods to enliven activist cultural events and street protests? MaxZine describes Eggplant Faerie events as "armed with the three lavender shields of fun, friendly, and unexpected."[117] This is a strategy to get lots of people to show up for protests and other social justice gatherings, says MaxZine, noting that it's hard to motivate people unless they know they'll have fun.

Why not have fun? Some of my friends work their asses off for crappy wages. Others are busy putting in gardens, building houses, salvaging materials, taking care of people with illness, and turning compost piles. People get tired and don't always want to give more of themselves if they don't think it's going to change things anyway. Millions protested the [first] Gulf War, and George Bush [the First] ignored them in his video game of mass murder, convincing my generation that protest doesn't affect politics much in the age of cyber-surrealism. My friends love parties; so, the object is to draw people to demonstrations by promising that

---

117 MaxZine Weinstein, "Radical Faerie Activism. Part One of Two."

they'll have fun. That's where the outfits, stilt-walking, creative propaganda, juggling, and make-up come in handy.

The Eggplant Faerie Players' satirical performance as Ladies For Nasty Art (LANA) is one early example of their street theater style. The EFP's first couple of years touring (1989 to 1990) coincided with a big cultural controversy over freedom of expression in art. Pressured by Congress, the National Endowment for the Arts (NEA) canceled shows and grants due to artistic content, including grants to performance artists Karen Finley, Tim Miller, John Fleck, and Holly Hughes who became known as the NEA 4.

In 1990, the Eggplants were passing through MaxZine's former home of Ann Arbor during the Ann Arbor Street Art Fair, which is attended by hundreds of thousands of people each year. Inspired by the satire group Ladies Against Women, they decided to attend in character as Ladies Against Nasty Art. Armed with a flyer detailing the group's demands, they toured the fair. LANA, led by SPREE decked out in a very tasteful Lily Tomlin-esque ensemble, went to each booth and dramatically praise any art that did not offend family values, such as a landscape painting, and threw a fit if there were any nudes in the art. MaxZine wrote about this action:

> Everyone was surprised. Most laughed at the satire. Some stared in shock, some pulled their children away, some wanted extra copies of our literature. My favorite people are the ones who act like nothing unusual is happening. Or those who took it all so literally and tried to figure out why men in dresses (some of whom had beards) were opposed to lewd art. As people experienced the unexpected, they generally warmed to our friendliness...we were friendly and non-confrontational, which drew people in to find out more. Humor has a way of breaking down barriers and helping people open their minds.[118]

---

118 Ibid.

In another example of creativity in protest space, in 1996 MaxZine mobilized a group of about twenty-five people from IDA and the surrounding Homo Hollow to join the protests against construction of the Watts Barr nuclear power plant in East Tennessee. On the anniversary of the Chernobyl disaster, they held a "Miss Nuclear Meltdown" Pageant at the protest, with a dozen contestants including Backwards Betty (with breasts growing out of her back), Miss Three-Eyed Myland, Barbarella Thunder Thighs, and The Three-Headed Boy. There were two people on stilts to present a headdress that looked like a cooling tower as a grand prize—when that headdress caught fire from its sparklers, it caused hilarious spontaneous mayhem—and the crowd loved it.

In more recent years, MaxZine and others in the IDA neighborhood have built an ongoing relationship with the Oak Ridge Environmental Peace Alliance, which organizes regular vigils and protests. After attending a few of those protests, the Eggplant Faerie Players started performing for the Peace Alliance's events.

Oak Ridge, Tennessee (a few hours from IDA) was built as a secret city during WWII, one of two places that the bombs dropped on Hiroshima and Nagasaki were developed. Called "Atomic City," it is still a site of building and retrofitting nuclear weapons. There is a creek that runs by the nuclear weapons facility and through a black neighborhood, with signs that say not to go near the water. When the Peace Alliance held a three-day training for nonviolent protests skills, the people from IDA offered to cook a meal for them and present it as dinner theater, called "Dinner at the Chez Guevara." While trainers and trainees ate, groups of performers would go around to tables singing songs or doing little skits, and everyone remembers it as great fun. For MaxZine, situations like this—conferences or meetings—are her favorite way to perform, where the Eggplant Faerie Players can make skits that speak to whatever the group is focused on and offer satire of what's being addressed, offering a chance for humor and fun even when the issues are very serious.

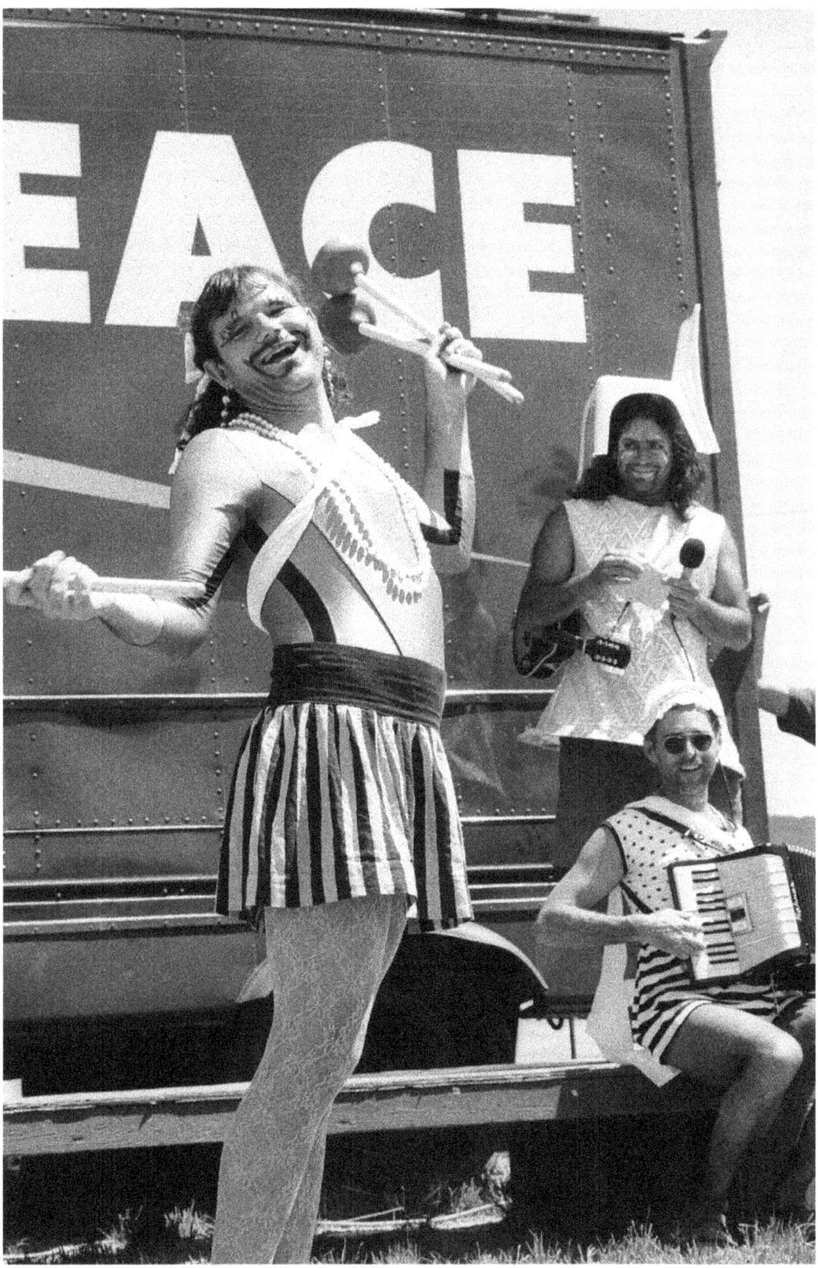

Eggplant Faerie Players protest and perform at Watts Barr nuclear power plant, 1996
(Photo credit: Keith Gemerek)

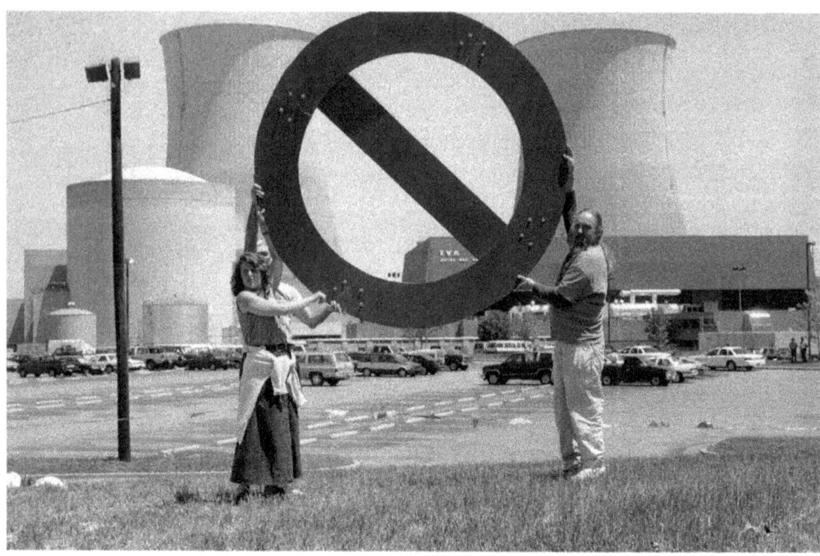

Eggplant Faerie Players protest and perform at Watts Barr nuclear power plant, 1996 (Photo credit: Keith Gemerek)

In my conversations with the Eggplant Faeries, much of the group performance storytelling ends as the '90s came to a close, however Max-Zine and TomFoolery have continued to perform together as the Eggplant Faerie Players, using a vaudeville circus format, including a 2012 tour called *Welcome to Homo Hollow: 17 Years of Queer Country Living Celebrated through Music, Satire, Juggling, and Drag.*

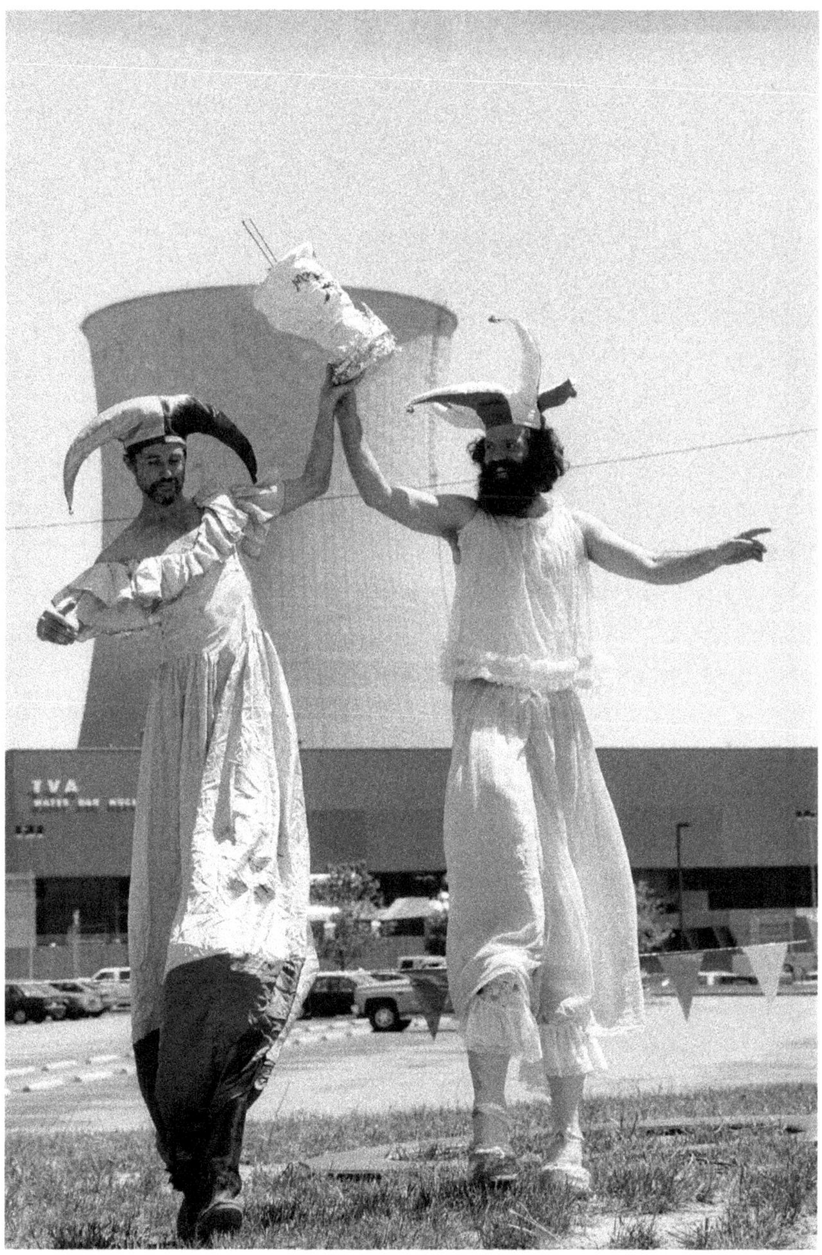

Eggplant Faerie Players protest and perform at Watts Barr nuclear power plant, 1996
(Photo credit: Keith Gemerek)

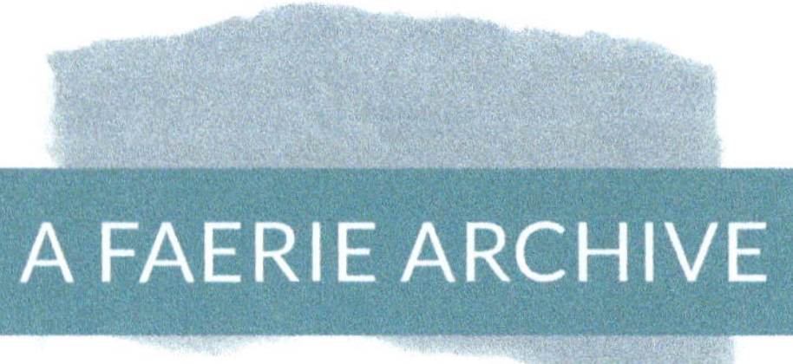

A FAERIE ARCHIVE

In 2010, I started digging through the IDA and Eggplant Faerie Player archives as part of my tasks at a week-long work party. Much of the history of the Eggplant Faerie Players has disappeared because they lived in a valley where mold and mildew destroy paperwork and electronics. There are very few old scripts available, very little video documentation—most of these pieces of the archive have been lost to moldy trash piles over the years. I spent many days going through IDA's files, scanning any photos, flyers, and articles I could find, and gathering dusty old VHS and Hi-8 tapes of Eggplant Faerie performances and IDA gatherings, and later I secured a mini-grant from the San Francisco-based Feyboy Arts Collective to cover the costs of digitizing and editing those tapes. This gave me the opportunity to watch *Person Livid with AIDS*, a highlight reel of scenes from multiple shows, and the 1997 Night of 1000 Stars gathering.

In 2012, research for this project also brought me to the William Way LGBT Community Center's archives[119] in Philadelphia to read through the back issues of *Radical Faerie Digest* (*RFD*) in search of write-ups on the Eggplant Faerie Players. *RFD* is a quarterly "reader written journal for gay people which focuses on country living and encourages alternative lifestyles."[120] Founded in 1974, it was originally "a country journal for gay men[121] everywhere." Still publishing today, each *RFD* issue has

---

119   The John J. Wilcox, Jr. LGBT Archives.
120   For more information, see: http://www.rfdmag.org/.
121   Or, some issues say "faggots."

a different title based on the acronym, including Rustic Faerie Dreams (Fall 1974), Really Feeling Divine (Spring 1975), Raving Flamer's Diary (Fall 1975), Recruiting Feminist Drakes (Fall 1977), Revolutionary Faggot Desire (Winter 1978), Retrospective For a Decade (Summer 1984), Rushed For Deadline (Spring 1994), and on and on.

I started at the beginning, paging through glorious reports, debates, photos, poetry, and more. I found myself reading issues from the late '70s and early '80s with both a feeling of wonder and sorrow—look at what these gay men were talking and thinking about! An issue devoted to the "Faggots and Class" conference; an issue on ageism; gay men writing about their relationships with women; the humor issue! These issues are full of content that feels so wholesome to me: rural living details, plant medicine, kitchen-queen recipes. . . . And then there's simultaneously a full range of politics being explored around identity, privilege, and survival, including discussions of how people feel about being called or calling themselves "faggot" and "sissy," and exploration of "Sissie Effeminism" as a specific Radical Faerie feminism.

Why did I feel sorrow browsing this archive? I knew AIDS was coming. As I opened the first 1981 issue I felt myself growing tense, wondering how and when in the '80s AIDS would emerge in the pages of this journal—when would AIDS awareness reach country queers, and how would it change their culture? I said something about this to the man I was sharing a table with, a retiree who volunteers at the archive three days a week. We had a moment of acknowledging together that we can't really do anything in a gay archive without thinking about the impact of AIDS. He was organizing brochures from LGBT groups and said he kept being reminded of people he lost. It was a relief to name that heaviness, witness for each other, and even laugh about it together.

It turned out that the Center's *RFD* archives ended mid-1994, but as I was leaving, I ran into a Faerie friend who offered for me to come to his house and check out his personal collection, which covered most issues since the mid-'90s. A few days later I was tucked away in his drag closet/reading room going through many of the later issues, reading articles and seeing so many gorgeous photos of queers—many of whom I have met through being part of Faerie communities. I noticed my mind wandering as I paged through, spinning off into fantasies of life in Faerieland. From my room at the top of the stairs, I overheard a conversation about a poz sex party,[122] and later I was so charmed when my viewing-experience was enhanced by the sounds of gay sex floating through the hall, a perfect soundtrack to the pages and pages of photos of dicks in nature. The whole experience brought me to thoughts of Eric Rofes' crucial books *Reviving the Tribe: Regenerating Gay Men's Sexuality and Culture in the Ongoing Epidemic* and *Dry Bones Breathe: Gay Men Creating Post-AIDS Identities and Cultures*. I was witnessing and immersed in the longer story of Radical Faerie Culture, before, during, and after the Plague Years.

I was looking at this history and simultaneously feeling and imagining my own possibilities, and feeling jubilation in the gay sex and glamour happening around me as I read. Reading these journals left me feeling more whole; they reminded me of the people I love in this culture, the long story of how it came to be, and that who I am has a place within Faerie framework and culture.

122　For HIV-positive gay men.

CONCLUSION

I knew that the stories of the Eggplant Faerie Players and Jenny Romaine were important to document in their own right; as my research deepened, I suspected another dimension of meaning would emerge from looking at the stories together.

In writing people's history-style profiles of these artists, I also came to understand myself as a kind of *zamler*,[123] collecting fragments of their creative ethnographies. How could I remix these fragments, practicing the methodology I was learning about, in my own work? I realized that I needed to not only put the pieces of the stories in a metaphorical room together, but also to bring the artists together in person to meet each other and have conversations about their work, their strategies, and their cultures. But which "land" could host such a gathering? It seemed easiest for Jenny and me to travel to Tennessee, where so many Eggplant Faerie Players live in the same neighborhood and Jenny and I could have a woodland getaway. Jenny was excited about the idea, and we all agreed on a five-day stretch to gather together at IDA in October 2012.

---

123 Yiddish: amateur collector, archivist.

Getting all of us in a room together wasn't easy. As the dates approached, I scrambled unsuccessfully to find a ride for Jenny and myself from the Northeast to Middle Tennessee. With all the logistical *tzuris* (aggravation) between travel plans and personal calendars, I was unsure if the details weren't lining up because it wasn't meant to be, or if it was just about making it work. I kept thinking of a dream I'd had a few months earlier, a precarious journey through narrow roads at night to IDA, how I woke up thinking about the word *mitzrayim*—the "narrow spaces" we talk about escaping each year at Passover, on the path towards our liberation.

Jenny told me, "Look, it's a miracle I was able to carve out these five days. So we'll take the bus! It's Sukkos and it's traditional to go on a supernatural pilgrimage, so this is like a classic Yiddish journey!" Then we realized we could do traditional Sukkos water libations at IDA's waterfall. Thinking of the epic bus trip as our hero's journey made it fun again, and our plans took shape.

A SUPERNATURAL SUKKOS ADVENTURE

We took the bus. On our layover in Washington, DC, we tried to watch the first 2012 presidential debate using the bus station's spotty Wi-Fi. No luck, just short snippets of the conversation between long, glitchy pauses. It was surreal, as if our Yiddish supernatural travels couldn't fully receive the 2012 political dispatches. Waiting for the bus to Nashville, the woman behind us in line was three-quarters of the way through Ayn Rand's *The Fountainhead* and her constant silent smirk was strangely menacing. Jenny was wearing a bright blue unisuit jumper, a string of giant pearls, and had her hair up in two high pigtails. I was wearing all black, more aware of my in-between gender outside of my subcultural bubble. We left a friend a birthday phone message in English and Yiddish. I grew more and more aware that we were extremely visible as queer Jews.

Finally, fifteen hours later, we reached IDA. The smell of the woods was intoxicating. That first night, all the residents and visitors collaborated to make two sheets of pizza, as we all huddled in the kitchen for warmth. Ingredients included homegrown shiitake mushrooms, tomatoes, squash, peppers, onions, garlic, oregano, basil, and mozzarella cheese that Jenny brought with her from New York. This was the first of many moments that weekend where a seemingly empty kitchen suddenly manifested a feast by what seemed like magic. I watched Jenny and MaxZine and SPREE get to know each other, laughing and joking and making long strings of puns, figuring out who they knew in common from ACT UP New York and other performers and activists. The next day, Jenny and I hiked to a waterfall with IDA's canine companions, and observed the Sukkos ritual of water libations. Next, we visited with Merril Mushroom—fabulous longtime area resident, Jewish lesbian, sci-fi writer, and (we learned) daughter of a famous Punch and Judy puppeteer. The next morning, we visited friends up the hill from IDA, met their baby chickens, and ate a feast of duck eggs, garlic broad beans, sweet potato pancakes and pear sauce from their land and IDA's gardens. On the last day of our visit, MaxZine came home from a stilt-walking gig with ingredients for us to make everything bagels from scratch together.

We looked through photo albums. I went through the archive collections and took photos of some documents that hadn't been scanned yet. We helped out in the IDA gardens—filling up big bags with bright orange and yellow marigold heads that would be fermented later for mead.

During our visit, I interviewed SPREE and MaxZine in the kitchen building and the front house (where their rooms were located), in a living room decorated with wigs and telephones that SPREE used as Barbara Broadcast. I interviewed Jenny in the area near IDA's back barn, where SPREE's Magic Day had taken place. We talked sitting on big flat rocks in the creek near a swimming hole, and then moved to a sunny spot in the back gardens near a rose arbor. During the interview, we were visited by bright red cardinals, a yellow finch and other bird friends.

In our final interview, Jenny Romaine shared something she learned from her friend and collaborator Jennifer Miller, and I found myself laughing with the shock of its clarity. "We're not weird," she said, "the rest of the world is weird."

> Capitalism's weird. We're just artists, we're clowns, we're thinking people. We're whoever, but we're not running around destroying people's lives and incarcerating people and stopping and frisking them. . . . Our queer world, where there is what Rachel Mattson calls this "queer political desire," has a limitless, non-normalized, very very open utopian vision of what's possible. . . . When we do our goofy funny stuff that we love, in the show we're the center of the world and we get to define what's normal, and we get to turn the rest of the world on its ear.

The Eggplant Faerie Players' group interview seemed to materialize organically—like the magical feasts that generated daily out of collective kitchen witchery. After our visit with Merril on our second day at IDA, Jenny and I watched MaxZine, TomFoolery, and their friend Knuckles practice the current version of the Eggplant Faeries' ever-evolving show, *Welcome to Homo Hollow*. Sandy Katz joined the audience with a visiting friend. We sat in the sun on tables that transform into benches, and I snacked on treats that Merril had dropped off, gathered from neighbor Sister Soami's local dumpster-diving bounty. As we watched juggling and musical acts on the lawn between the front house and the kitchen, another group of residents and guests installed roofing on a new shed structure. The dogs napped at our feet.

After the rehearsal, the group conversation shifted to Eggplant Faerie history, and we were just starting to talk about the show *Dial M for Mothership* when MaxZine exclaimed "Here comes the Mothership now!" A crew of former Eggplants had arrived: Dashboard, Junebug, and Leopard. I hadn't known they could make it over for dinner, or that TomFoolery could stay for the interviews! We set up at the kitchen table and *kibitzed* while a growing stream of people showed up—friends from around the "homo hollow" gathered for good stories and manifested a deluxe meal including a variation on a classic Yiddish dish, *kasha varnishkes*, made with homegrown shiitakes and renamed "kashiitakes."

This group interview was a frenetic and hilarious conversation between a group of friends, housemates, neighbors, and collaborators of twenty years around a kitchen table, while more friends and neighbors cooked a massive feast a few feet away—audibly, my recording of the interview is total chaos, and it beautifully reflects the joy, collectivism, and humor of the culture we were documenting.

It was a cold night, but the abundance of love, food, stories, and the humor of longtime creative collaborators in the room was so warming. I marveled at how we make all of this out of nothing—we gather, again and again, and in gathering we make and remake a culture. We are diasporic people, traveling the edges of the mainstream, and the lands we conjure through gathering and through performance are places we need for healing from the traumas of those border-crossings, the narrow spaces we travel towards liberation.

PLACE MATTERS

I wanted to learn about the places Yiddishland and Faerieland merged and overlapped, the transformative strategies generated from the spaces in-between. In bringing these artists together, I saw clearly that place matters—both the material places where the artists live their daily lives, and the different conjured cultural spaces of Yiddishland and Faerieland.

Jenny is a New Yorker who has made a life as a full-time artist. She understands herself as a worker, rooted in labor justice politics—she is completely professional about her methodology and practice. She struggles to figure out how to pay her rent given the reality that performing arts funding has tanked in the current economy, and that the weirdness of her work can be a barrier to funding when curators say things like "It's amazing! But is it really *theater*?"

The Eggplant Faeries have made an off-the-grid life in rural land projects, and though they do get occasional paying gigs by touring colleges or community centers, they mostly earn whatever income they live on through other means. Their group identity includes a puckish kind of playful pride about being unprofessional, and insisting that they're "just making it up as they go along" and "who cares if people get it"—as in Leopard's comment "maybe we didn't want to be got." They laugh about reviews that call their work self-indulgent.

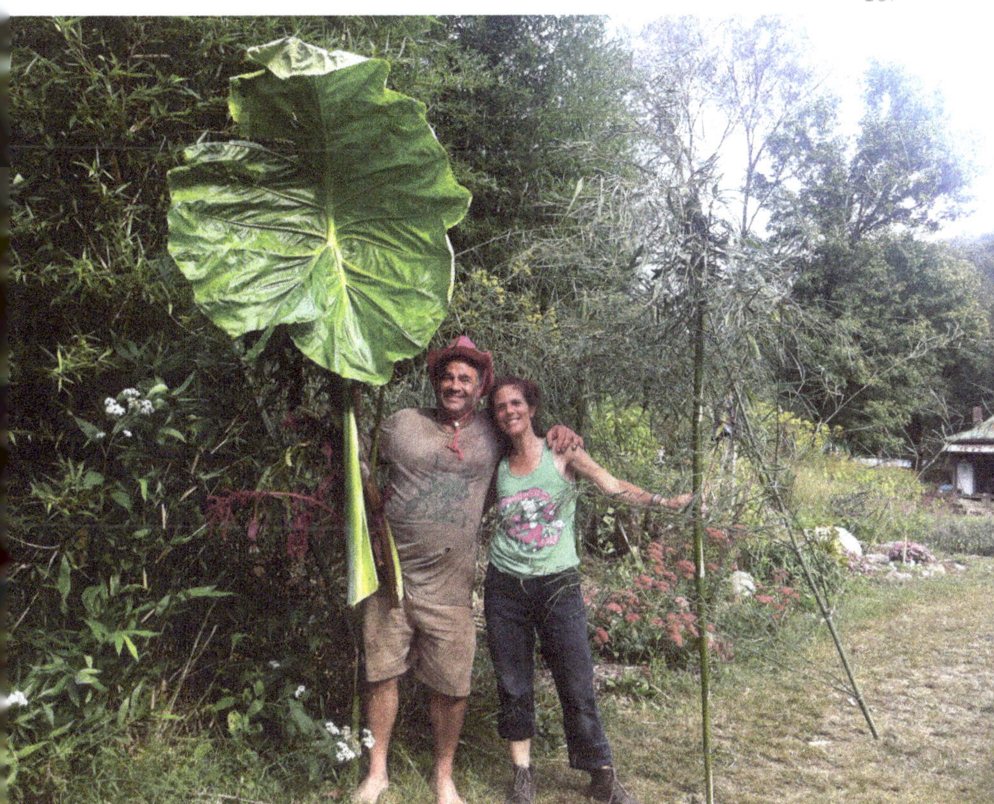

MaxZine Weinstein and Jenny Romaine, Idyll Dandy Arts 2013

I found myself wondering if the way that the Eggplant Faeries are light-hearted about their unprofessional productions, while Jenny is so clearly professional in her process, might be related to the different ways that men and women are treated by the larger world of theater—and specifically the way that queer women are explicitly marginalized in the professional theater world of New York.[124] I also think this might be one of the big differences between living in Yiddishland and living in Faerieland. The history of theater in Yiddishland is so developed—there are so many theatrical styles, structures, stars, scholars . . . it's a very rich landscape including many different ways to be a professional ex-perimental theater-maker. In contrast, the recent history of theater in Faerieland is about scrappy, goofy performances at rural gatherings

124 I'm thinking about Sarah Schulman's writing about this in *Stagestruck: Theater, AIDS, and the Marketing of Gay America* (Durham: Duke University Press, 1998).

with hastily thrown-together free-box drag. The ancient Faerie-fool's role is about undermining oppressive structures through strategic misdirection and illuminating reflection, it's a performance of not taking power (or anything) seriously. The Fool's role is to be unpredictable—unprofessional—and to invoke chaos that moves people to anger, laughter, or other feelings that shatter the structures of business as usual.

While Jenny understands herself as a cultural worker in a legacy of creative labor, and the Faeries understand their performance as purposefully unprofessional, their productions have a lot in common. Both often make shows that invite anyone who wants a role to participate—no experience necessary—and we all get to choose our own roles. They both attempt big visions with little rehearsal-time, building many shows out of cardboard and recycled elements of their previous productions. They both perform on the streets, at protests, wherever people gather—and rarely on formal stages. For how different their processes may be, the end results don't look entirely different. In both cases, fun matters. Jenny says, "The interest in the project is to experience joy" and "Fun is not just for fundamentalists." Eggplant Faerie Player Leopard says,

> The Eggplant Faerie Players was nothing like I had been involved with before…Eggplant, while dealing with serious subjects, particularly AIDS, just had a sort of irreverence. I think that was what made it "faerie" as much as anything. Just how much joy and irreverence was to be found.

Jenny expresses her connection to the archive of Jewish culture very clearly. The Eggplant Faerie Players, on the other hand, talk less explicitly about the ancient queer traditions they draw from. Still, their trickster nature, their love of wordplay, their references to the role of the "sacred clown," and even their name demonstrates roots in this history. Judy Grahn explains the radical role of faeries and drag queens in her book *Another Mother Tongue*, which explores the origins of gay culture:

> Sensual, barbed, informative, revolting, political—Fairy speech
> is a living art. . . . The drag queen is like the king's jester without
> the king, some theatrical combination of the Fool, the Hanged
> Man, and the Empress all rolled into one and without a true
> territory. . . . Their usual character of speech is a spewing of a
> running stream of advice, predictions, protection, commentary,
> gossip, "truth-saying." . . . And using the ancient chaotic powers,
> Gay trickster queens of all descriptions keep the matrix of hu-
> man thought in the disrupted, tumultuous state that prevents
> stagnation and keeps true creativity and flexibility possible.[125]

Though "Eggplant" may be a happy accidental acronym for Emma Goldman Gypsy Players Annual National Tour, it also evokes purple, that
queerest color—associated throughout history with homoeroticism,
androgynous and transgender people, and the transitional spaces on
the horizons, between worlds.

I like to say that Jenny Romaine makes queer art about Jewish culture
and the Eggplant Faerie Players make Jewish art about queer culture.
Although this generalization doesn't cover the totality of their work, it's
a dynamic that plays out in many of their stories. The Eggplant Faeries' show *Next Year in Sodom* and Jenny Romaine's backward-marching
KlezKanada event are great examples of this dynamic. "Marching backwards," says Jenny, "that's queer."

The Eggplant Faeries talk about the "three lavender shields of fun,
friendly, and unexpected" that enable them to get away with bringing
radical and challenging politics from the margins to the mainstream.
Jenny Romaine talks about "Truth in Gay Clothes"—adding glitz and
glamour as a strategy to enable sharing radical truths that would shut
conversation down if not presented with some of Parable's fancy drag.

---

125 Grahn, 231.

All of their work is rooted in the legacies of Jewish and queer cultures that have long struggled against repression, oppression, and many facets of trauma. They are informed by anti-capitalist, anti-militarist, and anti-assimilation politics. Trying to share their politics could easily get heavy-handed. "I know if I get preachy, watch out." says MaxZine, "It gets dangerous and didactic very quickly. And you lose people." Instead, their work is spectacular, carnivalesque, deliciously shocking, rapturously disorienting.

Jenny talks about "role-modeling principled disobedience." MaxZine says that "part of our anarchistic theatrical process is that we each decide what roles we want to do."

In these two theater worlds, we practice working collectively. We "train to be better at hearing and seeing people." We perform alternative worlds, alternative endings to stories, exploring the edges of our political and cultural desires. We practice "being revolting"—performing revolutionary moments. We actually practice winning our struggles for justice, and learn what it feels like. This helps us recommit to the struggle to get there in our "real lives."

These artists resist assimilation, but it's not about rejecting tradition. Instead, they demand the right to dialogue with their traditions, proclaiming that Fundamentalist and Orthodox communities—those with conservative and nostalgic relationships to the traditions—don't own the legacies. These artists remix traditional stories, rituals, and aesthetics—recycling and re-arranging the historical fragments (or we could say "queering" them) into newly relevant, evolving culture. The pieces are fragmented because our world is imperfect. Our histories need this retroactive healing power, this practice of rearranging our attention, as much as our futures need the new ways of perceiving that our remixing can generate.

May this work be a blessing on the memory of Ha!, Eggplant Faerie Player and longtime IDA resident, whose deeply radical, joyful, irreverent spirit is so present in this Faerieland archive; and who taught that "being empowered means being powerful in one's own right, of having the spiritual strength to make and manage personal change." [126]

And may this work be a blessing on the memory of Adrienne Cooper, whose contributions to the cultural resilience of Yiddishland are immense, profound, and inspirational; who wrote that she loved Yiddish for "hard-to-describe delights, for the rage it brings to injustice, for its wonderful weight on the tongue, for the arc it forms between poles of Jewish identity—from otherworldly to this worldly, from grit to grace—and for the astonishing ushpizin, unexpected guest spirits, who show up and have what to say."[127]

---

126 Thank you to Socket Klatzker for sharing this with me from a personal letter. Ha! died on February 24, 2008 at the age of sixty. Socket also shared that Ha! chose his name so that he would be called upon while his friends were laughing.
127 From the liner notes to Cooper's 2010 CD, "Enchanted: A New Generation of Yiddishsong."

Acknowledgments

Incredible gratitude to Jenny Romaine and to all of the Eggplant Faeries who shared their stories, insights, and lives with me and who inspire me so deeply.

Thank you to Karen Pittelman for helping me figure out the scaffolding to support the story-telling, and to Corina Dross for excellent copyediting, indexing, and feedback. Thank you also to Katt Lissard, Caryn Mirriam-Goldberg, S.B. Sowbel, and Lise Weil, with whom I wrote this book in so many different drafts and pieces, in the Goddard College Transformative Language Arts Program.

Big love to all of the following and more for conversations, giving feedback, sharing stories, and otherwise informing my sense of possibility about this work: Ari Maxwell Bachrach, Chris (Lady B) Bartlett, Mattilda Bernstein-Sycamore, Eric Bunting, Annie Danger, J Dellecave, Corina Dross, Dan Fishback, Matty Hart, Marissa Johnson-Valenzuela (Thread Makes Blanket Press), Socket Klatzker, Debora Kodish, Daniel Rosza Lang/Levitsky, Sloan Lesbowitz, Elan Margolis, Rachel Mattson, Femmy Rose, Anna Elena Torres, Rachael Sterner Nepon, Kate Sorensen, Cleo Woelfle-Erskine.

Thank you to photographers and artists who shared their images with me for this project, including Virginie Danglades, Mor (Mornography) Erlich, Bugz Fraugg, Keith (Fussy) Gemerek, Rosin Bean James, Alan Lankin, Peter Lien, Minister Erik McGregor, Betsy Nepon, Jombi Supastar, and Richard Termine.

Works Cited

"About Divan." *Pálinka Pictures*. Accessed April 26, 2012. http://www.palinka-pictures.com/divan_about.html.

"About Us." *Living Traditions: Community-Based Yiddish Folk Culture*. Accessed April 26, 2012. http://www.livingtraditions.org/docs/about.htm.

Anzaldúa, Gloria, and AnaLouise Keating. *The Gloria Anzaldúa Reader*. Durham: Duke University Press, 2009.

"Back to School with the Lesbian Avengers, 1992." *YouTube* video, 4:15, posted by kellysansculotte on September 10, 2012. Accessed April 28, 2013. http://www.youtube.com/watch?v=dzIbGdP7MDQ.

Barry, Lynda. *Cruddy: An Illustrated Novel*. New York: Simon & Schuster, 1999.

Bell, John. "The Miniature a Sprout Spaghetti Dinner." *Vimeo*, a collection of five videos. Accessed May 22, 2013. http://vimeo.com/album/1785053.

Berger, Joseph. "Adrienne Cooper, Yiddish Singer, Dies at 65." *New York Times*. December 28, 2011. Accessed June 2, 2013. http://www.nytimes.com/2011/12/29/arts/music/adrienne-cooper-expert-on-yiddish-music-is-dead-at-65.html.

Bleyer, Jennifer. "'City of Refuge.'" *The New York Times*. March 18, 2007. Accessed April 26, 2012. http://www.nytimes.com/2007/03/18/nyregion/thecity/18hasi.html.

"Bread and Puppet: Cheap Art and Political Theater | Puppeteers and Sourdough Bakers of Glover." *Bread and Puppet*. Accessed April 26, 2012. http://breadandpuppet.org.

Clifford, James. *The Predicament of Culture: Twentieth-Century Ethnography, Literature, and Art*. Cambridge, Mass.: Harvard University Press, 1988.

Dashboard, Tom Foolery, Leopard, Sandor Katz, Junebug, and MaxZine, interviewed by author on October 4, 2012 at Idyll Dandy Arts, Dowelltown TN. Tape recording.

de Garron, Agnes. "Agnes Knows." *Radical Faerie Digest* 65 (Spring 1991), xx.

De St. Croix, Lisa. "Next Year in Ramah." *Zuni Mountain Sanctuary*. Accessed September 6, 2012. www.zms.org/stories/fall98/nextyear.html.

"Eggplant Faerie Players Perform at Appalachian State University Nov. 17." *Appalachian State University News*. November 10, 2007. Accessed November 8, 2012. http://www.news.appstate.edu/2000/11/10/eggplant.

Ehren, Christine. "La MaMa *Gluckel of Hameln* Adds Two Performances Feb. 12 & 13." *Playbill*. January 27, 2000. Accessed April 26, 2012. http://www.playbill.com/news/article/50293-La-MaMa-Gluckel-of-Hameln-Adds-Two-Performances-Feb-12-13.

Fishman, David E. *The Rise of Modern Yiddish Culture*. Pittsburgh: University of Pittsburgh Press, 2005.

Goldman, Emma. *The Social Significance of the Modern Drama*. Boston: R.G. Badger, 1914.

Gottesman, Itzik Nakhmen. *Defining the Yiddish Nation: The Jewish folklorists of Poland*. Detroit: Wayne State University Press, 2003.

Graham, David M. "Gay channel surfing and satire." *The Michigan Daily*, November 16, 1994. Accessed September 8, 2012. http://news.google.com/newspapers?id=7k45AAAAIBAJ&sjid=ayUMAAAAIBAJ&pg=2878%2C16399474

Grahn, Judy. *Another Mother Tongue: Gay Words, Gay Worlds*. Boston: Beacon Press, 1984.

"Great Small Works: Introduction, History, and Company Bios." *Great Small Works*. Accessed April 26, 2012. http://www.greatsmallworks.org/pages/about_the_company.html#history.

Gross, Rebbetzin Hadassah. "Truth in Gay Clothing (or: Why I Wear Designer Couture)." *The Hadassah Gross Blog*. May 11, 2004. Accessed April 28, 2013. http://hgross.blogspot.com/2004/05/truth-in-gay-clothing-or-why-i-wear.html.

How to Survive a Plague. Directed by David France. California, Culver City. 2012. Film.

"Idyll Dandy Acres." *Vimeo* video, 23:22, posted by The Hussin Brothers. Posted March 8, 2011. Accessed May 22, 2013. http://vimeo.com/20793515.

Jeffreys, Joe E. "An Outre Entree into the Para-ridiculous Histrionics of Drag Diva Ethyl Eichelberger: A True Story" (PhD diss., New York University, 1996).

Kaplan, Esther. "Political Funeral." *Movement Research: Performance Journal* 7 (September 1993, States of the Body).

Kassow, Samuel D. *Who Will Write Our History?: Rediscovering a Hidden Archive from the Warsaw Ghetto.* New York: Vintage Books, 2009.

Kramer, Larry. "1,112 and Counting." *New York Native* 59 (March 1983).

Lecker, Michael. Transcription of "History of the Faeries." *It Was Curiosity | The Notes of a Cultural Studies Student.* January 23, 2012. Accessed February 17, 2013. http://itwascuriosity.wordpress.com/2012/01/23/transcription-of-history-of-the-faeries.

"Mad Dr. Science, Trying Not To Be Bitter, Leaving Loved: SPREE Vance reflects on the emotional rollercoaster of living with AIDS. As told to Sandorfag and transcribed by Susan Stoddard." *Radical Faerie Digest* 86 (Summer 1996): 42-43.

Mattson, Rachel. "What Can Jewish Be?" Accessed April 25, 2012. *JBooks.com.* http://www.jbooks.com/interviews/index/IP_Mattson_Romaine.htm.

Moore, Patrick. *Beyond Shame: Reclaiming the Abandoned History of Radical Gay Sexuality.* Boston: Beacon Press, 2004.

Nettles, "Eggplant Faerie Players Profile," *Radical Faerie Digest* 114 (Summer 2003, Radically Fine Designers).

Rofes, Eric E. *Dry Bones Breathe: Gay Men Creating Post-AIDS Identities and Cultures.* New York: Haworth Press, 1998.

---. *Reviving the Tribe: Regenerating Gay Men's Sexuality and Culture in the Ongoing Epidemic.* New York: Haworth Press, 1996.

Romaine, Jenny. Interviewed by Pauline Katz, August 24, 2011 at KlezKanada, Montreal. Video. Yiddish Book Center, Wexler Oral History Project.

---. "Jenny Romaine on Shtetl." *Shtetl on the Shortwave.* 90.3 FM, CKUT, March 5, 2010. Accessed April 28, 2013. http://shtetlmontreal.com/2010/03/05/jenny-romaine-on-shtetl.

---. "Political Funerals in the Context of the AIDS Crisis" (MA thesis, New York University, 1993).

Ryzik, Melena. "A Playful Occupy Halloween Trots Out the Puppets." *Culture and the Arts - ArtsBeat Blog - NYTimes.com.* October 28, 2011. Accessed April 25, 2012. http://artsbeat.blogs.nytimes.com/2011/10/28/a-playful-occupy-halloween-trots-out-the-puppets/#.

Safran, Gabriella. *Wandering Soul the Dybbuk's Creator, S. An-Sky.* Cambridge, Mass.: Belknap Press of Harvard University Press, 2010.

Schulman, Sarah. *Stagestruck: Theater, AIDS, and the Marketing of Gay America.* Durham: Duke University Press, 1998.

Schweizer, Yaron (Nettles) interviewed by Sarah Schulman, October 17, 2004. ACT UP oral history project, interview 61. New York: New York Lesbian & Gay Experimental Film Festival, 2006. http://www.actuporalhistory.org/interviews/images/nettles.pdf.

Shandler, Jeffrey. *Adventures in Yiddishland: Postvernacular Language and Culture.* Berkeley: University of California Press, 2005.

Shapiro, Gary. "Great Small Works Moves From P.S. 122." *The New York Sun.* January 10, 2006. Accessed April 26. 2012. http://www.nysun.com/arts/great-small-works-moves-from-ps-122/25579.

"Sharing & Caring | interview with MaxZine Weinstein." *David Sheen | documentarian & designer.* Accessed November 8, 2012. http://www.davidsheen.com/sharing/interviews/maxzine.htm.

Smulyan, Shayn E. "The SoCalled Past: Sampling Yiddish in Hip-Hop," in *Choosing Yiddish: New Frontiers of Language and Culture,* 357-376. Detroit: Wayne State University Press, 2012..

Solomon, Alisa. "A Yiddishe Mama Courage." *Village Voice.* January 18, 2000. Accessed April 26. http://www.villagevoice.com/2000-01-18/theater/a-yiddishe-mama-courage.

"Some Excerpts from the Memorial Service for Adrienne Cooper." *Jewish Currents.* February 19, 2012. Accessed June 2, 2013. http://jewishcurrents.org/some-excerpts-from-the-memorial-service-for-adrienne-cooper-9201.

SPREE, interviewed by author. Tape recording. Idyll Dandy Arts, Dowelltown TN, October 5, 2012.

SPREE, interviewed by Sarah Schulman, October 16th, 2004. ACT UP oral history project, interview 60. New York: New York Lesbian & Gay Experimental Film Festival. 2006. http://www.actuporalhistory.org/interviews/images/SPREE.pdf.

"SPREE de Corps." *POZ: Health, Life & HIV* 27 (September 1997). Accessed November 8, 2012. http://www.poz.com/articles/244_1747.shtml.

Tamarkin, Jeff. "The Klezmatics Bio." Accessed December 14, 2015. http://klezmatics.com/about/bio.

"Text of Megillah" from Jewish Holidays and Festivals on *Chabad.org.* Accessed April 25, 2012. http://www.chabad.org/holidays/in-depth/default_cdo/aid/39643/jewish/Megillah-Commentary.htm.

"Thirty Years of HIV/AIDS: Snapshots of an Epidemic." *amFar, The Foundation for AIDS Research*. Accessed April 28, 2013. http://www.amfar.org/thirty-years-of-hiv/aids-snapshots-of-an-epidemic.

Van Gelder, Lawrence. "Theater Review; Motherly Advice in Yiddish With Historical Asides." *The New York Times*. February 1, 2000. Accessed April 25, 2012. http://theater.nytimes.com/mem/theater/treview.html?res=9f01efd8163ff932a35751c0a9669c8b63.

Weinstein, MaxZine interviewed by author, October 5, 2012 at Idyll Dandy Arts, Dowelltown TN. Tape recording.

Weinstein, MaxZine interviewed by Sarah Schulman, October 16, 2004. ACT UP oral history project, interview 59. New York: New York Lesbian & Gay Experimental Film Festival, 2006. http://www.actuporalhistory.org/interviews/images/weinstein.pdf.

---. "Radical Faerie Activism. Part One of Two" *AGENDA: Monthly Independent News and Culture around Ann Arbor* (March 1999). Accessed September 8, 2012. http://www-personal.umich.edu/~lormand/agenda/9903/06.pdf.

---. "Radical Faerie Activism. Part Two of Two." *AGENDA* (March 1999). Accessed September 8, 2012.
http://www-personal.umich.edu/~lormand/agenda/9903/14.pdf.

---. "Faerie Theater." *AGENDA* (April 1999). Accessed September 8, 2012.
http://www-personal.umich.edu/~lormand/agenda/9904/15.pdf.

Wex, Michael. *Born to Kvetch: Yiddish Language and Culture in All of Its Moods*. New York: St. Martin's Press, 2005.

Williams, Lena. "600 in Gay Demonstration Arrested at Supreme Court." *New York Times*. October 14, 1987. Accessed April 28, 2013. www.nytimes.com/1987/10/14/us/600-in-gay-demonstration-arrested-at-supreme-court.html?page.

"YIVO Institute for Jewish Research | About YIVO." *YIVO Institute for Jewish Research*. Accessed December 16, 2015. https://www.yivo.org/About-YIVO.

Index

www.ingramcontent.com/pod-product-compliance
Lightning Source LLC
Chambersburg PA
CBHW050003040726

47599CB00014B/1187